Recipes from Pasquale's Kitchen

Recipes from Pasquale's Kitchen

Pasquale Carpino

Judith Drynan

Doubleday Canada Limited, Toronto, Ontario   1984
Doubleday & Company, Inc., Garden City, New York

Library of Congress Catalog Card Number 84-10251
ISBN 0-385-19306-8
ISBN 0-385-19307-6 (pbk.)

Typeset by Q Composition, Toronto, Ontario
Printed and bound in Canada by Gagne Printing Ltd.
Artwork by Janet Wilson

A Summerhill Press Book
Summerhill Press Ltd., Toronto, Ontario

Canadian Cataloguing in Publication Data
Carpino, Pasquale, 1936-
    Recipes from Pasquale's kitchen

Includes index.
ISBN 0-385-19306-8 (bound). — ISBN 0-385-19307-6 (pbk.)

1. Cookery, Italian.   I. Title.

TX723.C38 1984   641.5945   C84-098781-1

Library of Congress Cataloguing in Publication Data
Carpino, Pasquale, 1936-
    Recipes from Pasquale's kitchen

    Includes index.
        1. Cookery, Italian.   I. Title
TX723.C296   1984   641.5945   84-10251
ISBN 0-385-19306-8
ISBN 0-385-19307-6 (pbk.)

CONTENTS

FOREWORD

When I first came to North America as a young man, I was fortunate that there were so many opportunities for chefs, particularly for those trained in Europe. But there were also some difficulties, and one of these was trying to recreate the dishes I had learned to cook at home. It was impossible to reproduce the authentic taste of Italy using North American ingredients, as many Italian chefs soon found out. In some cases the right ingredients were not available, and when they were, the taste and texture were often very different. One had to adapt, be creative, and learn to cook in a new way.

So now I am always amused when I see cookbooks offering authentic Italian regional recipes. I do not try to mislead you. What I want to give you is "North American cooking with an Italian fantasy". You will be able to cook glorious meals using only those ingredients which are readily available in your area. It makes no sense to spend money on expensive imported goods, especially when the local products are superior in many cases. For example, I think the prosciutto which is cured here is much better than that imported from Italy, because of the excellent pork produced by Canadian farmers. Also, I prefer the local pasta made with high quality Durham wheat to the imported variety. People should be proud to use these products, and not be fooled by the claims of superiority in imported foods.

In this new book, I offer you a collection of my favorite recipes. Many are from my television program, "La Cucina Italiana con Pasquale", some are traditional favorites, and the rest are new recipes created especially for this book, but they all have one thing in common — they are simple to cook. They are "la cucina casalinga" or "made for cooking at home".

To cook something beautiful and share it with others, is one of the most satisfying experiences there is, and when you prepare food at home, you manage to add something special because you know the people you are cooking for. It allows you to be creative and artistic as a chef, and believe me, this is appreciated by the ones you love, because this personal quality is something they will never find in a restaurant.

I am giving you these recipes from my own kitchen so that you can prepare them for your family and friends. I hope you will enjoy cooking them as much as I have enjoyed sharing them with you.

Pasquale

Buon'appetito!

APPETIZER
Antipasto

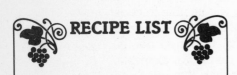
Antipasto means "before the pasta", although the two courses are hardly ever served at the same meal.

At an Italian dinner, the *antipasti* are the appetizers — sometimes specific dishes, and sometimes just a bit of this-and-that to nibble on before the main course. The purpose of the antipasto is to take the edge off our hunger and soothe our senses so that we can appreciate the food which comes after, but this doesn't mean that a well-prepared appetizer can't be delicious as well.

A popular antipasto tray consists of foods which are fresh and in season, different types of sausages sliced thinly, cheeses, and pickled vegetables — all arranged artistically on a large platter. Small plates and eating utensils should be provided, and then people can serve themselves. Some ingredients to keep on hand are:

Acciughe—anchovies
Capocollo—cured pork, sliced thinly
Carciofini all'Olio—artichoke hearts in olive oil
Oliva—green and black olives
Peperoncini—sweet red or green peppers
Pimenti—sweet red peppers
Provolone—cheese cut in thick pieces
Prosciutto—air-dried Italian ham sliced wafer-thin
Salami—spicy Italian sausage, sliced thinly
Salsiccia secca—dry pork sausage, sliced thinly
Sardine—sardines

As you will see from the recipes which follow, many other antipasto dishes are favorites as well, including stuffed eggplant and eggs, and baked clams and oysters.

Polpette di Riso

Fried Rice Balls

These rice balls are fun to eat, because of the way the cheese pulls out in strings after each bite.

Ingredients	Regular	Metric
Rice	1 1/2 cups	375 ml
Oil	2 tbsp.	30 ml
Onion, chopped	1	1
Green pepper, chopped	1	1
Pork, cut in small pieces	8 oz.	250 g
Chicken livers, chopped	2 oz.	50 g
Mushrooms, sliced	6	6
Tomato, peeled and chopped	1	1
Red wine	2 oz.	50 ml
Parmesan cheese, grated	4 oz.	50 ml
Mozzarella cheese, chopped	6 oz.	200 ml
Parsley	2 tbsp.	30 ml
Salt	1/2 tsp.	2 ml
Pepper	Pinch	Pinch
Eggs, lightly beaten	6	6
Flour	4 oz.	125 ml
Breadcrumbs	1 cup	225 ml
Oil for frying		

1. Cook rice and set aside.
2. Heat oil in a frying pan and cook onion and green pepper for 5 minutes. Add meat, livers and mushrooms, and cook for another 5 minutes, then add tomato and wine and simmer for 10 minutes.
3. Take off the heat and add the cooked rice, cheeses, parsley, seasonings and 2 of the eggs. Mix well and form into egg shapes with the palms of your hands.
4. Dip into flour, then beaten egg. Coat thoroughly with breadcrumbs and deep-fry at 375°F./190°C until golden brown. Drain on paper towels and serve.

Serves 6-8

Aperitifs/Aperitivo

Aperitifs stimulate the appetite, so they are the perfect way to start a meal. Here are three of the most popular Italian aperitifs.

Asti Spumante. A sweet, sparkling wine from the region near the town of Asti in northwestern Italy. Made from the Muscat/Moscato grape, it is Italy's version of champagne, but with a beautiful bouquet and taste all its own.

Campari. This red, bittersweet drink is defined as a spirit instead of a wine because of its higher alcohol content. It is made from herbs and citrus, and is most often mixed with soda water and a slice of lemon.

Vermouth. This fortified wine, flavored with various herbs, spices, seeds and barks, is usually made with a base of Muscat wine. You can buy it sweet or dry, red or white, depending on your preference. Then drink it by itself, or use it as a mix, the way dry white vermouth is added to gin to make a martini.

Antipasto di Mare
Seafood Appetizer

This cool and delicious appetizer can be prepared in advance and left to marinate in the refrigerator until ready to use. Any meaty fish, like squid, lobster, or octopus, can be substituted for the cuttlefish.

Ingredients	Regular	Metric
Cuttlefish	8 oz.	250 g
Shrimp	8 oz.	250 g
Fennel or celery, thinly sliced	1/2 head	1/2 head
Green pepper, sliced	1	1
Tomato, chopped	1	1
Juice of 1 lemon		
Olive oil	2 oz.	50 ml
Capers	2 tbsp.	30 ml
Parsley, chopped	1 tbsp.	15 ml
Wine vinegar	1 tbsp.	15 ml
Oregano	Pinch	Pinch
Salt	1/2 tsp.	2 ml
Pepper	Pinch	Pinch

1. Simmer cuttlefish in lightly salted water for 10 minutes. Cool and drain.
2. Cook shrimp for 3 minutes in unsalted water. Cool and drain.
3. Cut cuttlefish into thin slices, and place in a large bowl with all the other ingredients. Toss well.
4. Chill in the refrigerator for at least 2 hours before serving.

Serves 4-6

Cuttlefish

The cuttlefish is in the mollusc family, and is a close relative of the squid and octopus. It is famous not only for its taste, but for the ink it squirts out when it is frightened or startled. This ink is used in sepia paint, and accounts for the fish's Latin name — Sepia Officinalis. The cuttlefish is popular in the entire Mediterranean, but particularly in Italy where it is usually beaten before being eaten. Don't worry, though. You can generally find it all cleaned and ready for cooking at any good fishmonger.

"A good antipasto tray depends on what is in season, what is in the refrigerator, and what is in the cook's imagination."

Pane Aglio

Garlic Bread

This is my special way to make garlic bread. It's also a good method of using up any slightly dry bread you might have.

Ingredients	Regular	Metric
Sour cream	2 tbsp.	50 ml
Soft butter	6 tbsp.	90 ml
Garlic cloves, minced	2	2
Parmesan cheese, grated	4 tbsp.	60 ml
Paprika	1 tbsp.	15 ml
Bread, Italian or French	12 slices	12 slices

1. Preheat oven to 400°F./200°C.
2. Mix the sour cream, butter, garlic, cheese and paprika together in a bowl, and spread on the bread slices.
3. Cook in the oven until the topping starts to bubble and brown, then serve immediately.

Serves 4-6

➤ *To make garlic butter, place peeled and quartered garlic cloves in a bowl of soft butter and leave, covered, for 4 hours. Then discard the cloves, and use the butter.*

Antipasti Vegetali

Any vegetables can be marinated and used as appetizers, if they are cut in attractive shapes, and all the pieces are the same size. Use carrots, eggplant, zucchini, cauliflower or broccoli spears, mushrooms and tiny onions.

Put some oil in a frying pan and add about 1 pound of cut-up vegetables. Cook very quickly, shaking the pan, for about 5 minutes, then put in a bowl, and cover with 1 cup of olive oil, 1/2 cup of wine vinegar, 1 clove of peeled garlic, a pinch of salt and oregano, and 4 peppercorns. Cover and let sit for 4 to 24 hours, then drain and serve.

Fritto Misto

Many vegetables are delicious dipped in batter and deep-fried, and when several are served together, the dish is called Fritto Misto di Vegetali. As well as zucchini, vegetables which can be cooked this way are green beans, eggplant slices, small mushroom caps, rings of green pepper, asparagus tips, cauliflower or broccoli flowerets, and artichoke bottoms and hearts.

Be sure to have the vegetables thoroughly dry before dipping in the batter, and it's a good idea to let the batter sit on the vegetables for 5 or 10 minutes so it can dry a bit before cooking. This way it will be crisper and more golden.

▶ *The secret of successful Fritto Misto is hot oil – make sure it is between 350°F. and 375°F. before adding the ingredients. To save time before serving, fry up all the vegetables ahead of time, drain, and just before eating, heat them in a 350°F. oven for 15 minutes.*

Zucchini Fritti

Fried Zucchini in Batter

Select the smallest zucchini you can find, and serve this great finger-food appetizer with your favorite dip.

Ingredients	Regular	Metric
Zucchini	6	6
Water	2 cups	500 ml
Flour	2 cups	500 ml
Oil for frying		
Salt	1	1

1. Wash zucchini and trim ends. Cut into sticks 2"/5 cm long and ½"/1 cm thick.
2. Put water in a bowl and gradually whisk in flour until mixture has the consistency of mayonnaise.
3. Heat oil to 375°F./190°C, or until a cube of bread turns golden brown almost immediately.
4. Dip zucchini sticks in batter and lower into the oil with a slotted spoon. When golden on all sides, remove and drain on paper towels.
5. Continue until all the zucchini is done, then arrange on a heated platter and sprinkle with salt.

Serves 4-6

Cipolle Frite con Pastella

Onion Rings

Sweet slices of onion coated with batter and deep-fried until golden. Nice as an appetizer, but serve immediately after frying so they will be crunchy.

Ingredients	Regular	Metric
Spanish onions	2	2
Salt	1/2 tsp.	2 ml
Pepper	Pinch	Pinch
Eggs, beaten	4	4
Flour	4 tbsp.	60 ml
Oil	4 tbsp.	60 ml

Cold water	6 oz.	200 ml
Baking powder	1 tbsp.	15 ml
Oil for frying		

1. Peel onions and cut into rounds ½"/1 cm thick. Separate into rings and place on a tray. Sprinkle with salt.
2. Add salt and pepper to beaten eggs and stir in the flour, oil, water, and baking powder. Mix well and let sit for 10 minutes. Mix again and then dip onion rings in the batter until they are thoroughly coated.
3. Heat oil in a pot or deep fryer to 375°F./190°C and cook onion rings until light golden. Remove and drain on paper towels. Serve immediately.

Serves 4

Vitello Tonnato

Veal with Tuna Sauce

Since this dish is served chilled, it can be made well in advance and refrigerated until ready to use. A nice summer dish.

Ingredients	Regular	Metric
Veal, roasted and sliced	12-18 slices	12-18 slices
Capers, chopped	2 tbsp.	30 ml
Green onions, chopped	3	3
Anchovies, chopped	6	6
Mayonnaise	1 cup	250 ml
Juice of 1 lemon		
Tuna fish, drained	6 oz.	200 g

1. Place veal slices on a large platter.
2. Make sauce by combining remaining ingredients and mixing or blending until smooth.
3. Spoon sauce over veal and refrigerate. Garnish with tomato and lemon slices and serve.

Serves 4-6

▶ *The best onions to use for fried onion rings are mild ones like the Bermuda, Spanish or Italian, because of their very juicy, very thick layers.*

Mayonnaise/Maionese

This beautiful and adaptable sauce can either be made by hand, beating the oil in with a wire whisk, or more conveniently, in a blender.

For complete success, all the ingredients should be at room temperature, and you can even rinse the bowl or blender jar with hot water before using. If making by hand, put in a bowl:

   2 egg yolks
   1/2 tsp. dried mustard or Dijon
   Pinch of cayenne
   1 tsp. vinegar or lemon juice
   3/4 cup olive or vegetable oil

Whisk the first 4 ingredients until blended and light yellow. Then add the oil, drop by drop, whisking constantly.

When the sauce begins to thicken, you can add the oil a little more quickly, and stop holding your breath. As soon as all the oil has been incorporated, taste carefully, frown thoughtfully, and then adjust the seasonings.

If using the blender, make exactly the same way except use one egg yolk and one whole egg. Put the speed on high, and add the oil slowly.

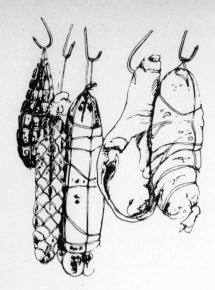

Cured Italian Meats

Italians make some of the best cured meats in the world. Most of the varieties are made from different parts of the pig, and are salt-cured and air-dried. Here are several of the most popular types.

Prosciutto. This is raw salted ham and a specialty of many parts of Italy, but especially Parma. In fact, the most famous type is *prosciutto di Parma*, or Parma ham.

A leg of pork is salted and turned evenly for 30-60 days so that the salt is distributed evenly, then it is washed and hung to air-dry in a warm breeze for a week. After that, it is hung in progressively cooler air for the next 12 months.

The result is one of the finest cured hams in the world, and is delicious sliced very thinly and served with fresh figs or slices of ripe sweet melon.

Before buying, ask the butcher to give you a taste so you can choose your favorite.

Capocollo. This is a delicately smoked salt-cured ham which is similar to prosciutto except that it is made from the pork shoulder, and so has less fat. It is usually sliced thinly and used as an appetizer.

Pancetta. Similar to North American bacon, although is more spicy and hot. Can be cut in strips or cubes for cooking and adding to various recipes.

Antipasto Misto
Mixed Italian Appetizer

A mixed antipasto is one of the most popular first courses in Italy. This particular version includes a selection of pickled vegetables, as well as sliced meats and cheeses.

Ingredients	Regular	Metric
Anchovies, drained and filleted	6	6
Capocollo, sliced thinly	8 slices	8 slices
Salami, sliced thinly	8 slices	8 slices
Prosciutto, sliced thinly	8 slices	8 slices
Green olives	4 oz.	125 ml
Pickled carrots	4 oz.	125 ml
Pickled mushrooms	4 oz.	125 ml
Celery stalks, sliced lengthwise	4	4
Red pepper, sliced	1	1
Green pepper, sliced	1	1
Fontina cheese, sliced thinly	8 slices	8 slices
Asiago cheese, sliced thinly	8 slices	8 slices
Parsley sprigs	8	8
Boiled eggs, cold	8 halves	8

1. Arrange the ingredients on a large platter and garnish with the parsley and egg halves.
2. Put the platter in the middle of the table and let everyone serve themselves.

Serves 4-6

Funghi al Aceto

Pickled Mushrooms

This makes a good addition to mixed Italian antipasto.

Ingredients	Regular	Metric
Mushrooms	1 lb.	500 g
Onion, sliced thinly	1/2	1/2
Salt	1/2 tsp.	2 ml
Pepper	Pinch	Pinch
Olive oil	2 oz.	50 ml
Juice of 1 lemon		
Wine vinegar	2 oz.	50 ml

1. Trim the hard stems off the mushrooms, then place the mushrooms in a bowl with the onion and remaining ingredients.
2. Place in the refrigerator for 24 hours. Drain and serve.

Serves 4-6

> ► *Broiled fresh mushroom caps will be juicier if they are broiled with the hollow side up first, and the cap side up to finish.*

Mozzarella Fritta

Fried Mozzarella Cheese

Also called "mozzarella in carrozza" which means "in a carriage" and refers to the cheese enclosed in the bread slices.

Ingredients	Regular	Metric
Olive oil	4 oz.	125 ml
Bread slices	8	8
Mozzarella cheese	12 oz.	375 g
Flour	2 oz.	50 ml
Eggs, beaten	2	2

1. Heat oil in a large frying pan.
2. Trim the crusts from the bread, and cut the cheese into 4 pieces the approximate size of the bread slices.
3. Place each cheese slice between 2 pieces of bread. Sprinkle with a little flour and dip into beaten egg.
4. Cook in hot oil until golden brown, turning once. Drain on paper towels and serve.

Serves 4

Mozzarella

Mozzarella is a cheese made from the milk of Italian cows, although it used to be made from buffalo milk. It is particularly good when heated because of its soft and slightly stringy texture, and is most widely used in the making of pizza and lasagne, on its own dipped in egg and fried, and in the very popular toasted sandwich, "mozzarella in carrozza".

It keeps well when wrapped tightly and refrigerated, but don't worry if a bit of mold develops on the outside. Simply cut it away, because underneath the cheese will be just as delicious.

Oyster/Ostriche

Oysters are one of the great gastronomic delights, and it was an Italian, Sergius Oraka, who first had the idea, in the 5th century, of creating artificial oyster beds.

Oysters can be eaten raw — or grilled as in Venice, with breadcrumbs, herbs, garlic, and olive oil.

The popular notion that they are an aphrodisiac is probably due to the fact that they are a sensuous food to eat, and also contain a large amount of vitamins and iodine which give the diner a feeling of health and well-being.

> ► *Usually, prosciutto is served sliced thinly, but in recipes like Uova con Prosciutto where it is chopped, a more economical way to buy it is to ask the butcher if he has any prosciutto ends. The meat is generally much reduced in price, and just as good to eat.*

Ostriche al Limone

Oysters and Lemon

Oysters like this are best swallowed whole. Just dip them in the sauce, pop them in the mouth, and down they go.

Ingredients	Regular	Metric
Oysters	24	24
Horseradish	1 tbsp.	15 ml
Sugar	1 tbsp.	15 ml
Tabasco sauce	6 drops	6 drops
Ketchup	4 tbsp.	60 ml
Juice of 1 lemon		
Salt	1/2 tsp.	2 ml
Pepper	Pinch	Pinch

1. Scrub the oysters very well, then open with an oyster knife and separate from the shell tops.
2. Discard tops and place bottoms on a large serving platter.
3. Mix other ingredients together and place in a small bowl for dipping.

Serves 6

Uova con Prosciutto

Stuffed Eggs with Prosciutto

Creamy egg yolks mixed with mayonnaise, prosciutto and capers, then placed in egg-white boats.

Ingredients	Regular	Metric
Hard boiled eggs, peeled	6	6
Onion, minced	2 tbsp.	30 ml
Prosciutto, chopped	1 oz.	50 ml
Mayonnaise	4 tbsp.	60 ml
Capers, chopped	2 tbsp.	30 ml
Tarragon	Pinch	Pinch
Salt	1/2 tsp.	2 ml
Pepper	Pinch	Pinch
Paprika	1/2 tsp.	2 ml

1. Slice eggs in half lengthwise and place yolks in a bowl.
2. Mash yolks and add all the other ingredients except paprika.
3. Fill whites with this mixture and sprinkle with paprika.

Serves 4-6

Melanzane Marinate

Marinated Eggplant

Eggplant sautéed with celery, onion, and garlic, then chilled in wine and vinegar.

Ingredients	Regular	Metric
Olive oil	1 oz.	50 ml
Eggplants, peeled and diced	2	2
Celery, diced	1 cup	250 ml
Onion, chopped	1	1
Garlic clove, chopped	1	1
Tomato paste	4 tbsp.	60 ml
Chicken stock or white wine	2 oz.	50 ml
Red wine vinegar	2 oz.	50 ml
Sugar	1 tsp.	5 ml
Salt	Pinch	Pinch
Pepper	Pinch	Pinch

1. Heat oil in a large frying pan, and cook and stir eggplant for 5 minutes. Remove and drain.
2. Add celery, onion, and garlic, and cook and stir another 5 minutes, adding a little more oil if necessary.
3. Stir in tomato paste, liquids, sugar, and the drained eggplant—simmer for 10 minutes, then taste, and add salt and pepper.
4. Chill for at least 1 hour, then serve.

Serves 4

Prosciutto e Melone

This is one of the simplest and most famous of all antipasto dishes, memorable for its unusual combination of tastes. Cantaloupe is the melon most often used, although honeydew is also good.

To select a cantaloupe which is perfectly ripe, look first at the bottom. It should have a tan indentation which is slightly sunken, with no bits of stem attached. The skin should look like a rough beige net, and have no green showing through.

Next — take a sniff. The fruit should smell sweet but not too fragrant, or else it might be over-ripe.

Finally, push your thumbs in gently at the top of the melon, not the stem end. A good cantaloupe should be soft but not mushy.

When you're ready to serve it, cut the melon in half and scoop out the seeds, then cut off the rind. Slice the fruit into thin crescents, and arrange them slightly overlapped on a salad plate.

For each person, use three or four thin slices of prosciutto, and lay them on top of the melon crescents.

Serve with lemon wedges, or freshly ground pepper.

SOUP
Zuppa

Soup is a complete food containing water, vitamins, minerals and protein, and very often the roughage needed to keep our bodies humming along efficiently. It is also a good choice for people on a diet or just being careful about their weight, because we tend to eat less on a day when we eat soup – perhaps because it's filling and satisfying.

Homemade stock is so good that it's a shame to use anything else, but canned stock may be substituted in a pinch, as long as it's not too salty.

Since Italian cooks are very practical, soups are also a source of economy. Every little bit of food is saved, and either used in the making of stock, or in the soup itself – to give the best possible taste without spending a fortune.

In Italy, soups are sometimes served instead of the pasta course. They are so filling that with a salad and some hot, fresh bread, they can provide a full meal. So be careful to balance the soup you serve with what goes after, or people might burst from too much goodness.

When you're making soup, it's a good idea to prepare more than you will need at one time and freeze the rest. Don't add any flour or thickening ingredients before freezing, though. When you're ready to eat it, just thaw and bring to a full boil as soon as it's defrosted. Then adjust the consistency and the seasonings, and serve. That way, you'll always have lovely homemade soup on hand when you need it.

Zuppa con Polpettini di Vitello

Soup with Tiny Veal Meatballs

Tiny meatballs are cooked right in the broth just before the soup is done.

Ingredients	Regular	Metric
Olive oil	3 tbsp.	45 ml
Garlic clove, minced	1	1
Onion, chopped	1	1
Celery stalks, chopped	2	2
Carrots, chopped	4	4
Tomato, peeled and chopped	1	1
Chicken stock	1 quart	1 L
Salt	1/2 tsp.	2 ml
Pepper	Pinch	Pinch
Ground veal	8 oz.	250 g
Eggs	2	2
Parmesan cheese, grated	1 tbsp.	15 ml
Flour	1 tbsp.	15 ml
Parsley, chopped	1 tbsp.	15 ml

1. Heat oil in a large pot and cook garlic and vegetables for 5 minutes.
2. Add stock and seasoning and bring to a boil, then lower heat and simmer for 45 minutes.
3. In a bowl, combine the meat, 1 egg, cheese, flour, and parsley, and mix well. Form into little balls the size of marbles, and drop into the soup 10 minutes before soup is done.
4. Just before serving, you can drop in 1 beaten egg, and stir gently until strands set. Serve immediately with grated cheese.

Serves 4-6

Chicken Stock/Brodo di Pollo

3 lb. chicken parts (wings, backs, necks)
2 carrots, cut in chunks
1 onion, peeled
1 clove garlic, peeled
2 celery stalks, cut in half
5 peppercorns
2 sprigs parsley

Wash the chicken and put in a large pot with the other ingredients. Cover with cold water and bring to a boil, then skim off the froth on top, lower the heat, and simmer for 45 minutes. Remove the cooked chicken meat from the bones and save for other uses. Return the bones to the broth and cook for another 2-3 hours. Strain and cool uncovered, then place in the refrigerator or freezer until the fat congeals on the surface. Now the fat can be removed easily. Use stock right away, or freeze in 1 or 2 cup containers for later use. If it is to be added to another dish, don't salt it.

Makes about 10 cups

► *Don't use strongly flavored vegetables in stock, because things like cabbage and cauliflower can overpower the other tastes.*

Crema di Cipolle e Patate

Cream of Onion and Potato Soup

This smooth, creamy soup of potatoes, onions and leeks is a good summer dish served cold.

Ingredients	Regular	Metric
Oil	2 tbsp.	30 ml
Leeks, whites only	2	2
Celery stalks, chopped	2	2
Onion, chopped	1	1
Chicken stock	1 quart	1 L
Potatoes, peeled and quartered	4	4
Heavy cream	2 cups	500 ml
Salt	1/2 tsp.	2 ml
Pepper	Pinch	Pinch
Parsley, chopped	1 tbsp.	15 ml
Shallot or green onion, chopped	1	1
Croutons	1 cup	250 ml

1. Heat oil in large pot. Split the leeks in two, wash thoroughly under running water and chop. Add to the pot with the celery and onion, and cook for 5 minutes.
2. Add stock and bring to a boil. Add potatoes and cook for 20 minutes until tender.

➤ *Foods which are to be eaten chilled will always taste less salty than when they were hot, so remember to add more seasoning when cooking, or taste and adjust before serving.*

3. Put mixture in a blender or push through a sieve until smooth. Return to pan, and stir in cream, salt and pepper. Cook for another 5 minutes or until soup thickens.
4. Serve hot with parsley, shallots and croutons on top, or chill for 2 hours and serve cold without the croutons.

Serves 4-6

Zuppa Crema di Funghi

Cream of Mushroom Soup

This elegant soup is a perennial favorite. Add a touch of sherry just before serving for a really special flavor.

Ingredients	Regular	Metric
Butter	4 tbsp.	60 ml
Mushrooms, sliced	1 lb.	500 g
Onion, diced	1	1
Celery stalk, chopped	1	1
Chicken stock	1 quart	1 L
White wine	4 oz.	125 ml
Nutmeg	Pinch	Pinch
Salt	1/2 tsp.	2 ml
Pepper	Pinch	Pinch
Flour	3 tbsp.	45 ml
Heavy cream	4 oz.	125 ml
Milk	2 cups	500 ml
Croutons	1/2 cup	125 ml

1. Heat the butter in a large pot and cook the mushrooms, onion and celery for 5 minutes.
2. Add stock, wine and seasonings and simmer for 10 minutes.
3. Mix the flour with the cream and milk until they form a smooth liquid, then bring the soup to a boil and whisk in the milky mixture.
4. Let cook for a few minutes, then adjust seasonings and stir in a spoonful of sherry if you wish. Serve with croutons sprinkled on top.

Serves 4-6

▶ *The most important thing to remember about fresh mushrooms is to keep them away from moisture. Store in a paper bag — never in plastic or a sealed container — as they must be able to "breathe" or they'll get soggy. To clean, wipe with a paper towel or a mushroom brush, or, if they're very dirty, rinse quickly under running water and dry immediately with paper towels, then cook uncovered.*

Fava Beans

Fava is Italian for broad bean, which, in Italy, is dried and used in soups. Fava beans belong to the family of legumes called pulses, which form one of the oldest known foods in the world. As well as being full of vitamins, they are high in natural fiber, and low in price. Although they have a slightly bland taste on their own, they make a perfect partner for spicy or salt-cured pork.

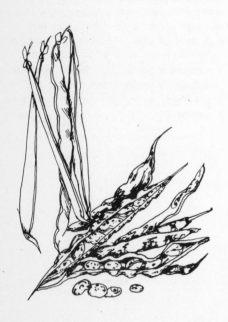

Zuppa di Fave

Fava Bean Soup

This is an old, traditional dish in Italy, and a distant cousin of "pork and beans". Any kind of pork will do for this—even bacon.

Ingredients	Regular	Metric
Olive oil	3 oz.	75 ml
Onion, chopped	1	1
Smoked pork, diced	4 oz.	125 ml
Garlic cloves, minced	2	2
Tomato, peeled and chopped	1	1
Salt	1/2 tsp.	2 ml
Pepper	Pinch	Pinch
Beef stock	1 quart	1 L
Fava beans, drained	19 oz. can	600 ml

1. Heat the oil in a large pot and cook the onion, pork, garlic and tomato for 10 minutes, stirring occasionally.
2. Add the seasonings, stock and beans and bring to a boil. Lower the heat and cook gently for another 20-30 minutes before serving.

Serves 4-6

Pasta e Cavoli

Pasta and Cabbage Soup

This soup can be made with any kind of cabbage, but Savoy cabbage is best because of its delicate flavor.

Ingredients	Regular	Metric
Olive oil	3 tbsp.	45 ml
Bacon or pancetta slices, chopped	3	3
Onion, chopped	1	1
Garlic clove, minced	1	1
Celery stalk, chopped	1	1
Cabbage head, shredded	1/2	1/2
Chili pepper	Pinch	Pinch
Basil	Pinch	Pinch
Salt	1/2 tsp.	2 ml
Pepper	Pinch	Pinch

Chicken stock	1 quart	1 L
Stivaletti pasta, cooked and drained	4 oz.	125 ml
Parsley, chopped	1 tbsp.	15 ml
Parmesan cheese, grated	1 tbsp.	15 ml

1. Heat the oil in a large pot and cook the bacon, onion, garlic, celery, and cabbage for 10 minutes.
2. Add seasonings and stock and bring to a boil. Stir in the cooked pasta, lower the heat and simmer for 10 minutes. Just before serving stir in the parsley, and sprinkle with grated cheese.

Serves 4-6

Pasta e Fagioli

Ditali Pasta and Bean Soup

Although this famous dish is considered to be a soup, it is thick enough to eat as a main course.

Ingredients	Regular	Metric
Olive oil	2 oz.	50 ml
Onion, chopped	1	1
Garlic cloves, minced	2	2
Bacon slices, diced	4	4
Salt	1/2 tsp.	2 ml
Pepper	Pinch	Pinch
Chili pepper	Pinch	Pinch
Tomato paste	4 tbsp.	60 ml
Chicken stock	1 quart	1 L
Romano beans, drained	19 oz. can	600 ml
Ditali pasta	6 oz.	200 ml
Parsley, chopped	2 tbsp.	30 ml
Romano cheese, grated	4 oz.	125 ml

1. Heat oil in a large pot and cook onion, garlic and bacon for 5 minutes.
2. Add seasonings and stir in tomato paste.
3. Add stock and beans and simmer for 10 minutes.
4. Cook and drain pasta and add to soup. Simmer for another 10 minutes and serve with parsley and cheese sprinkled on top.

Serves 4-6

Pasta in Brodo

Literally this means "pasta in the broth", and it makes a delicious and filling soup. It's also a wonderful way to use leftover cooked pasta — just chop it up and add it to the soup at the last minute. All kinds of uncooked pasta shapes can be used as well. If you're making a minestrone or other thick soup, cook the pasta right in the broth, but for a clear soup, cook and rinse the pasta before adding it to the stock. Any small pasta can be used, but here are some of the most popular types.

Alphabetti (alphabets). Small pastas shaped in letters.

Ditali (thimbles). Pasta in tubes about 1/2" long, and 1/4" wide.

Lumachine (baby shells). A smaller version of lumaconi (jumbo shells).

Orzo (oats). Small pasta which looks like grain.

Stiviletti. Small-cut elbow macaroni.

Zuppa di Ceci

Chick Pea Soup

Chick peas, also known as garbonzos, are not only tasty, but also an excellent source of dietary fiber. They're good cold in salads, or hot—as in this delicious soup.

Ingredients	Regular	Metric
Olive oil	2 tbsp.	30 ml
Garlic clove, minced	1	1
Celery stalk, diced	1	1
Red onion, chopped	1	1
Sage	Pinch	Pinch
Nutmeg	Pinch	Pinch
Chicken stock	1 quart	1 L
Chick peas, drained	19 oz. can	600 ml
Salt	1/2 tsp.	2 ml
Pepper	Pinch	Pinch

1. Heat oil in a large pot and cook the garlic, celery and onion for 5 minutes.
2. Add the rest of the ingredients and bring to a boil. Lower the heat and simmer for 20-30 minutes. Serve immediately.

Serves 4-6

Risi e Bisi

Rice and Pea Soup

This famous Venetian dish is classified as a soup. Just wait! You'll be able to eat it with a fork.

Ingredients	Regular	Metric
Oil	1 tbsp.	15 ml
Butter	4 tbsp.	60 ml
Onion, chopped	1	1
Bacon or pancetta slices, chopped	2	2
Parsley, chopped	1 tbsp.	15 ml
Peas	2 cups	500 ml
Rice, uncooked	1 cup	250 ml
Chicken stock	1 quart	1 L

Salt	1/2 tsp.	2 ml
Pepper	Pinch	Pinch
Parmesan cheese, grated	4 oz.	125 ml

1. Heat oil and half the butter in a large pot. Cook the onion, bacon and parsley for 5 minutes.
2. Add peas and rice. Cook and stir until rice is translucent and well-coated.
3. Heat stock and add to the pan along with the salt and pepper. Bring to a boil, then lower the heat and simmer until stock is almost absorbed, about 20 minutes.
4. Stir in remaining butter and half the grated cheese. Serve with the rest of the cheese sprinkled on top.

Serves 4-6

Zuppa di Piselli

Pea Soup

To make this soup even heartier, add one cup of cooked rice five minutes before serving.

Ingredients	Regular	Metric
Oil	2 tbsp.	30 ml
Bacon or pancetta slices, chopped	6	6
Garlic clove, chopped	2	2
Celery stalk, chopped	1	1
Green onion, chopped	1	1
Peas	2 cups	500 ml
Salt	1 tsp.	5 ml
Pepper	1/2 tsp.	2 ml
Tomatoes, peeled and chopped	2	2
Chicken stock	1 quart	1 L
Croutons	1/2 cup	125 ml

1. Heat the oil in a large pot and cook the bacon, garlic, celery and green onion for 10 minutes.
2. Add peas, salt, and pepper and cook for another 5 minutes.
3. Add the tomatoes and chicken stock and simmer gently for 1 hour.
4. When soup has thickened, serve with croutons on top.

Serves 4-6

▶ *Risi e Bisi is a Venetian specialty which has become popular all over Italy. When cooking it, just shake the pan — never stir — so that the peas will remain whole and not get mushed up.*

Peas/Piselli

Peas are a wonderful vegetable – colorful, tasty, and full of nutrition and fiber. Luckily, they freeze well, so sweet young peas are available all year round.

Fresh pod peas are at their best in April and May. Look for very green pods, with fat peas inside. When you open the pod, the smell should be lovely and fresh, and if you rub two pods together, they should squeak. Usually, one pound of podded peas will give you one cup of peas.

Zuppa di Legumi

Vegetable Soup

This is a good place to use the vegetable scraps you saved from other recipes. Remember that a good cook never wastes anything in the kitchen.

Ingredients	Regular	Metric
Butter	3 tbsp.	45 ml
Garlic clove, chopped	1	1
Onion, chopped	1	1
Cauliflower head	1/4	1/4
Carrots, peeled	2	2
Celery stalks	2	2
Leek, washed thoroughly	1	1
Potato, peeled	1	1
Spinach	1 cup	250 ml
Tomatoes, peeled	2	2
Chicken stock	1 quart	1 L
Salt	1/2 tsp.	2 ml
Pepper	Pinch	Pinch
Cayenne	Pinch	Pinch
Parsley	1 tbsp.	15 ml
Parmesan, grated	1 tbsp.	15 ml

1. Heat butter in a large pot and cook garlic and onion for 5 minutes.
2. Wash and chop the vegetables. Add to the pot and cook for 5-7 minutes.
3. Add stock and seasonings, and cook gently for 30-45 minutes.
4. When ready to serve, stir in parsley. Spoon into bowls and sprinkle grated cheese on top.

Serves 4-6

► *Save the trimmings from vegetables, like the core and skin from tomatoes, the ends of beans and carrots and so on, and put them in a special container in the freezer. Do the same with chicken bones when you debone breasts, and when you have enough for a stock, simply take everything out of the freezer and make the stock as usual.*

► *Make enough soup at one time for two meals. The next day, add rice, pasta, left-over vegetables, fresh-chopped parsley or whatever you like for a whole new wonderful tasting soup.*

Minestrone

Country Vegetable Soup

A minestrone is a "big soup" which consists of a variety of seasonal vegetables, bacon, and pasta or rice. If you serve it with some Italian bread it can be the whole meal.

Ingredients	Regular	Metric
Stivaletti pasta	6 oz.	200 ml
Olive oil	3 tbsp.	45 ml
Onion, sliced	1	1
Garlic cloves, chopped	2	2
Bacon or pancetta slices, chopped	4	4
Leek, washed and chopped	1	1
Celery stalks, chopped	2	2
Potatoes, peeled and chopped	2	2
Cabbage head, chopped	1/2	1/2
Spinach, chopped	1 cup	250 ml
Tomatoes, peeled and chopped	2 large	2
Chicken stock	1 quart	1 L
Romano beans, drained	19 oz. can	600 ml
Salt	1/2 tsp.	2 ml
Pepper	Pinch	Pinch
Parmesan cheese, grated	1 cup	250 ml

1. Cook pasta. Drain and reserve 1 cup of pasta water.
2. Heat oil in a large pot and cook onion, garlic and bacon for 5 minutes.
3. Add vegetables and cook, stirring, for about 5 minutes.
4. Add pasta water, stock, and beans and cook for 40 minutes. Stir in cooked pasta 10 minutes before soup is done.
5. Sprinkle grated cheese on top and serve.

Serves 6-8

Minestrone

In the Middle Ages, many weary travelers found food and rest at the roadside monasteries. The good monks would always have a large pot of meat and vegetables simmering on the stove for their hungry visitors, and this mixture came to be known as a minestra, which in Latin means, "to serve".

This describes many Italian soups today, but none so accurately as minestrone, or "big soup", which has become the national soup of Italy.

Okra/Gombo

Okra is a popular vegetable in Mediterranean countries, as well as in the Southern United States, where soups made with okra are called "gumbo". The natural thickening ingredient in okra turns a soup into something like a stew, and noodles are wonderful for soaking up the juices.

► *If an okra dish gets too gummy, add a little white vinegar and lemon juice until it has a good consistency.*

Minestra di Pollo con Okra

Chicken Okra Soup with Noodles

The vegetables of the Mediterranean—tomatoes, green peppers, and okra—combine with chicken and noodles to make this thick and delicious soup.

Ingredients	Regular	Metric
Olive oil	2 oz.	50 ml
Onion, chopped	2	2
Garlic clove, chopped	1	1
Celery stalks, chopped	2	2
Green pepper, chopped	1	1
Okra, washed and diced	1 cup	250 ml
Chicken broth	1 quart	1 L
Chicken, cooked and diced	1 lb.	500 g
Tomatoes, peeled and chopped	1 cup	250 ml
Salt	1/2 tsp.	2 ml
Pepper	Pinch	Pinch
Egg noodles, cooked and drained	4 oz.	125 ml
Juice of 1 lemon		
Parmesan cheese, grated	4 oz.	125 ml
Parsley, chopped	2 tbsp.	30 ml

1. Heat oil in a large pot and cook onion, garlic, celery, green pepper and okra for 5 minutes.
2. Add broth, chicken, tomatoes, salt and pepper, and cook for 10 minutes.
3. Add noodles and stir in lemon juice. Let stand for 5 minutes, then sprinkle with cheese and parsley and serve.

Serves 6-8

Minestra di Manzo e Orzo

Beef Orzo Soup

The delicate flavors of leeks and celery mingle with the hearty taste of beef, beef stock, and tomato. Carrots add the flavor and color, and the orzo pasta gives this soup a final touch.

Ingredients	Regular	Metric
Oil	2 tbsp.	30 ml
Onion, chopped	1	1
Celery stalk, chopped	2	2
Leek , white chopped	1	1
Carrots, diced	2	2
Beef, diced	6 oz.	200 g
Beef stock or consommé	1 quart	1 L
Tomato paste	1 tbsp.	15 ml
Salt	1/2 tsp.	2 ml
Pepper	Pinch	Pinch
Orzo pasta, cooked and drained	1 cup	250 ml
Parsley, chopped	2 tbsp.	30 ml

1. Heat oil in a large pot and add onion, celery, leek, carrots and meat. Cook and stir for 5 minutes or until meat is browned.
2. Add stock, tomato paste, salt and pepper, and cook for 10 minutes.
3. Add pasta and parsley and cook for 5 minutes more. Check seasonings and serve immediately.

Serves 4-6

Beef Stock/Brodo di Manzo

4-5 lbs. beef shank or knee, including bone
2 oz. oil
2 carrots, cut in chunks
1 onion, cut in 4
2 celery stalks with leaves, cut in half
5 peppercorns
1 clove garlic
1 bay leaf
1 tablespoon tomato paste

Heat the oil in a large soup pot, and cook the meat and bones until they are thoroughly brown. Add the other ingredients, and cover with 4 quarts of cold water. Bring to a boil, and skim off the froth until it is white, then lower the heat and simmer partially covered and at a slow bubble for 2-3 hours. Strain, skim off the fat, then use right away or freeze for later use. Makes about 10 cups.

► To give beef stock or stew a deep rich color, hold a whole onion over the heat element with a fork until the skin is dark brown, then add it to the stock — skin and all.

Pane Cotto

Bread Soup

This simple recipe, which has been handed down over the ages, consists of bread added to a mixture of tomatoes, stock and seasonings.

Ingredients	Regular	Metric
Olive oil	4 oz.	125 ml
Garlic cloves, chopped	3	3
Chili pepper	Pinch	Pinch
Tomatoes, peeled and chopped	1 lb.	500 g
Italian bread	1 lb.	500 g
Chicken or beef stock	3 cups	750 ml
Salt	1/2 tsp.	5 ml
Pepper	Pinch	Pinch
Basil leaves	4	4

1. Heat half the oil in a pot and cook the garlic and chili peppers for 5 minutes.
2. Remove seeds from tomatoes, and add tomatoes to pot. Cook gently for 5 minutes.
3. Cut bread into small pieces and add to pot, along with the stock, salt, pepper, and whole basil leaves. Simmer 15 minutes more.
4. Remove from the heat, cover and let rest for 1-2 hours. When ready to serve, stir well and serve in individual soup bowls. Sprinkle a spoonful of oil on each serving, and top with freshly ground black pepper. Serve cold, luke-warm, or reheat and serve hot.

Serves 4-6

Zuppa di Asparagi

Asparagus Soup

This is a good way to use tough asparagus ends, saving the tips to eat separately as a vegetable.

Pane Cotto

Pane Cotto (bread soup) is traditionally served at Easter, and is also called *tridura*, a term which comes from the Roman Catholic word *triduum* referring to the three days of prayer which come before a religiously important occasion.

This version of Pane Cotto comes from Florence, and is one of the most famous and characteristic dishes of that town.

The bread used should be several days old so that it doesn't get too mushy. It should end up in bunches with the liquid all around it.

► *When cooking asparagus, cook up twice as much as you will need for one meal, and put the rest in the refrigerator. For a quick and delicious dish the next day, serve the chilled spears with a bit of mayonnaise, and a cold pasta salad.*

Ingredients	Regular	Metric
Asparagus ends	2 lbs.	1 kg
Potatoes	2	2
Leek, white only	1	1
Water	5 cups	1 1/4 L
Butter	2 tbsp.	30 ml
Salt	1/2 tsp.	5 ml
Egg yolk	1	1
Heavy cream	4 oz.	125 ml
Croutons	1 cup	250 ml

1. Wash asparagus under running water and scrape tough parts. Peel potatoes and cut into small pieces. Split leek and wash under running water, then slice white part thin.
2. Place vegetables in a pot and add the water. Boil, uncovered, for 10-15 minutes until tender.
3. Force the vegetables and liquid through a sieve, or put in a blender until smooth.
4. Return to the pot, add butter and salt and bring to a boil.
5. Beat the egg yolk and the cream together in a bowl, then add some of the hot liquid. Whisk this mixture into the soup and serve with croutons on top.

Serves 4-6

Croutons

If you have bread which is just starting to go a bit dry, a great way to use it is to make croutons.

First, preheat the oven to 375°F. Then, cut the bread, dry or fresh, into small cubes.

Heat olive oil and a garlic clove in a large frying pan, and toss the bread around in it until all the cubes are well-coated. Put them in the oven until they are golden, about 5 minutes, and serve with salads, soups, or as a garnish around roasts or any meat.

➤ *If you want to give croutons a special taste when serving in soup, put some freshly grated parmesan cheese in a bag, and shake the croutons vigorously while they are still hot from the oven — then add right away to the soup.*

Crema di Pomodori

Cream of Tomato Soup

Onions, tomatoes and seasonings combine with sour cream to make this favorite soup extra tasty.

Ingredients	Regular	Metric
Oil	3 tbsp.	45 ml
Onions, chopped	2	2
Tomatoes, peeled and chopped	4	4
Parsley, chopped	1 tbsp.	15 ml
Fresh basil, chopped	1 tbsp.	15 ml
Sugar	2 tsp.	10 ml
Salt	1/2 tsp.	2 ml
Pepper	Pinch	Pinch
Sour cream	1 cup	250 ml
Chicken broth	2 cups	500 ml

1. Heat oil in a large pot and cook onions for 5 minutes until they are soft and golden.
2. Add the tomatoes and next 5 ingredients. Simmer, covered, for 20 minutes.
3. Puree in a blender until smooth, then cool and stir in the sour cream.
4. Put the broth in the pan and add the tomato-cream mixture.
5. Bring the soup barely to a boil, so that the sour cream doesn't curdle, and serve immediately.

Serves 4

► To make peeling tomatoes very easy, place them in boiling water for about 1 minute or until the skins start to crack, then remove and plunge them into cold water. The skins will practically fall off.

Stracciatella

Egg Drop Soup

Stracciatella means "little rags" and that's exactly what the eggs should look like when they are stirred into the hot broth of this light, savory soup.

Ingredients	Regular	Metric
Oil	2 oz.	50 ml
Butter	1 tbsp.	15 ml

► When adding eggs to Stracciatella, make sure they are at room temperature, then put them in a bowl and beat with a fork just enough to combine the yolks and whites. Take the soup off the heat, and immediately add the egg mixture in a slow, steady stream holding the bowl about six inches above the pan. At the same time, take a fork in your other hand, and stir the eggs in with wide circles as the mixture hits the surface of the hot broth, so you get the long strings you want. After the eggs have been stirred in, you may then put the soup back on the heat for 1 minute at a gentle simmer before serving.

Green onion, minced	2	2
Garlic clove, minced	1	1
Chicken, diced	4 oz.	125 ml
Salt	1/2 tsp.	2 ml
Pepper	Pinch	Pinch
Chicken stock	1 quart	1 L
Eggs, lightly beaten	2	2
Parmesan cheese, grated	3 tbsp.	45 ml
Parsley, chopped	2 tbsp.	30 ml

1. Heat the oil in a large pot and cook the onion, garlic and chicken for 10 minutes, stirring frequently.
2. Add seasonings and stock, and bring to a boil. Lower heat and simmer for 10-15 minutes.
3. Just before serving, remove soup from the heat and pour the beaten eggs into the broth, stirring very slowly. When the eggs have set into strands, about 2 minutes, serve at once with parsley and cheese on top.

Serves 4-6

> ➤ *If you are adding herbs to a soup, like dill, mint or parsley, always add at the last minute just before serving.*

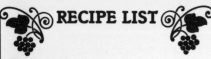
PASTA
and other pleasures

Pasta has become the national and traditional food of Italy, and although many other countries have noodles, Italians have taken this food beyond a simple staple and made it into an art form.

I like to call pasta the food of fantasy, because it gives the cook an opportunity to use freedom and imagination, and create a dish or recipe variation which is unique. There is practically no ingredient which isn't pasta's "best friend" and the different sizes and shapes are endless.

Pasta actually means "paste" — a paste made of water and hard wheat flour, with eggs sometimes added to make it tender. The Chinese were eating noodles way back in the Ming dynasty, but the first written record of it in Italy was in the middle of the 13th century.

It was always a dish which was served for "good" meals, and it wasn't until the middle 1800's and the invention of machines which could mass-produce pasta, that it became a daily food instead of something which was served on special occasions and feast days. Instead of making it commonplace, though, and taken for granted, it allowed people to be even more creative. Now there are literally hundreds of pasta recipes, and each region in Italy takes pride in its own way of preparing them.

In this section you will find recipes for pizza, risotto, gnocchi, and polenta, but mostly my favorite recipes for pasta and sauces. I hope that you will enjoy cooking and eating them so much that you will go on to invent your own.

Pasta all'Uovo

Homemade Egg Pasta

Pasta fresca, or fresh pasta, is usually made with eggs as well as flour and water. Make sure the flour has been ground from hard Durham wheat. The amount of water given is just a guide, since each batch of flour is different, and absorbs different quantities of liquid. Experiment until the consistency is just right.

Ingredients	Regular	Metric
Flour	4 cups	1 L
Eggs	4	4
Salt	1 tsp.	5 ml
Olive oil	2 tbsp.	30 ml
Warm water	4 oz.	125 ml

1. Put the flour on a table or counter and make a nest in the middle.
2. Break the eggs into the nest and add the salt, oil and some of the water.
3. Beat this mixture with a fork, and gradually incorporate the flour into the liquid, adding more water if necessary, until a thick pastry ball has formed.
4. Continue mixing with the hands until no more flour can be absorbed, and the dough doesn't stick to the counter. If the dough is the right consistency, you should be able to rub your hands together, and have the dough fall off easily in little balls.
5. Now, using a pasta machine, roll out the dough to the thickness you desire. Let the pasta rest for 30 minutes, then cut into required shapes.
6. Cook fresh pasta for 2-3 minutes in a deep pot of boiling salted water.

Makes 2 pounds

Cooking Pasta

You should always use a lot of water when cooking pasta, so that the surface of each piece is penetrated as quickly as possible, and the pasta cooks evenly without sticking together.

For each pound of pasta, bring 4 quarts of water to a rolling boil. Then add 2 tablespoons of salt unless the sauce is going to be a salty one, like anchovy, when you should just leave it out altogether. You can add a garlic clove to the water for extra taste, or a tablespoon of olive oil. This not only adds flavor, but makes the water boil faster. Some people believe it keeps the pasta from sticking together, but really, lots of water and stirring will do this better.

When the water is at a full boil, gradually add the pasta so the water keeps on boiling as vigorously as possible. If you're cooking homemade pasta, be sure and shake off any excess flour before adding the noodles, or the water will foam up and make a mess. When all the pasta is in the pot, stir it occasionally with a large fork until it's done.

Fresh pasta – *pasta fresca* – will be cooked in several minutes, or as soon as it rises to the top of the water, but dried pasta – *pasta secca* – will take longer. You must keep tasting it every couple of minutes to see if it is done.

The "bite" in pasta is very important, and pasta should always be cooked *al dente* which means "to the teeth". It should be soft but not mushy, and have a little resistance when you chew it.

When the pasta reaches this stage, drain it immediately in a large colander, and shake it around until all the water has gone. Now, a good way to improve the "bite" is to put the pasta back in the empty cooking pot on the heat, and toss it with a little butter and grated cheese. Or you can toss it with a spoonful of sauce until it is coated, and not quite white anymore. We call this *pasta macchiata*.

Pasta cools very quickly once it is cooked and starts to stick together, so make sure all your plates are hot, then add the sauce and serve the pasta immediately.

1. Place the flour on your counter in the shape of a small mountain. Make a large well in the center of the mound, break the eggs into it, and mix with a fork.

2. Mix all the flour into the egg. With your hands, begin blending all of the flour together, adding water if needed. Knead until the ball is smooth and elastic.

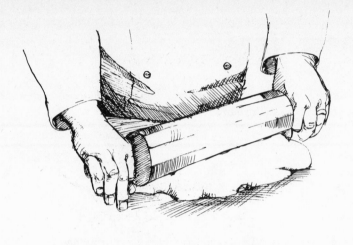

3. Roll the dough out with a roller into thin sheets. Sprinkle the board or counter with flour to prevent sticking.

4. Using the palms of your hands, roll up the dough for cutting.

5. Slice the dough into thin spaghetti, thicker fettucine, larger lasagna, or whatever thickness you wish.

> ➤ *If you are eating pasta with the family, you can pass a bowl of extra sauce so that everyone can help themselves. But if you have guests, serve them the extra sauce yourself, so that they will feel special.*

Pasta Verde
Green Pasta

This pasta is made just the same way as pasta all'uovo, except that cooked spinach is substituted for water.

Ingredients	Regular	Metric
Spinach	12 oz.	375 ml
Flour	4 cups	1 L
Eggs	4	4
Salt	1 tsp.	5 ml
Olive oil	2 tbsp.	30 ml

1. Take the stems off the spinach and rinse thoroughly.
2. Cook covered for 5 minutes without extra water, then drain well and press out as much liquid as you can. Chop finely until it looks like paste.
3. Now make pasta dough the same way as egg pasta, adding the spinach and a little extra water if necessary.

Makes 2 pounds

Salsa alla Marinara
Marinara Sauce

This red sauce is excellent with all kinds of pasta, and because it is meatless, it can also be served with fish and seafood.

Ingredients	Regular	Metric
Olive oil	2 oz.	50 ml
Garlic clove, chopped	1	1
Onion, chopped	1	1
Anchovies, chopped	8	8
Capers, chopped	2 tbsp.	30 ml
Basil	1 tsp.	5 ml
Red wine	6 oz.	200 ml
Chili pepper	1 tsp.	5 ml
Tomatoes, chopped	14 oz. can	450 ml
Tomato paste	3 tbsp.	45 ml
Parsley, chopped	1 tbsp.	15 ml

Salt	1/2 tsp.	2 ml
Pepper	Pinch	Pinch

1. Heat oil in a large pot and cook garlic and onion for 5 minutes.
2. Add the next 10 ingredients and simmer for 20-30 minutes.

Serves 4-6

➤ As a general rule, allow 8 oz. of pasta for four people as an appetizer, and 16 oz. as a main course, although if the pasta is served with a hearty sauce or stuffing, the amounts will have to be adjusted.

Salsa al Ragu

Meat Sauce

The meat for ragu should be cut in small cubes and browned quickly without scorching. This version with green peppers and celery, as well as tomatoes, is wonderfully tasty, especially with ribbed pasta.

Ingredients	Regular	Metric
Butter	2 tbsp.	30 ml
Olive oil	2 tbsp.	30 ml
Onion, chopped	1	1
Garlic cloves, chopped	2	2
Cubed beef	1 lb.	500 g
Green pepper, diced	1	1
Celery stalk, diced	1	1
Red wine	2 oz.	50 ml
Salt	1 tsp.	5 ml
Pepper	Pinch	Pinch
Basil	1/2 tsp.	2 ml
Tomatoes, undrained	28 oz. can	875 ml
Tomato paste	6 oz.	200 ml

1. Heat the butter and oil in a large pot, and cook the onion and garlic for 5 minutes.
2. Add the meat and cook and stir until it is nicely browned, then add the next 8 ingredients and simmer for 1 hour.

Serves 4-6

"Pasta is very impatient. The sauce will wait for the pasta, but the pasta won't wait for the sauce. So make sure your sauce is ready to go as soon as the pasta has finished cooking."

1. Mix together the dough as in the basic method. When you have a ball, begin to knead by passing through the widest roller setting.

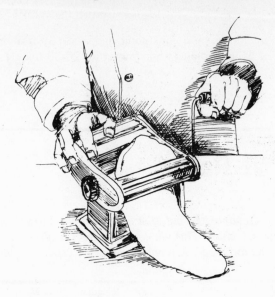

2. Fold the dough over once and pass through the rollers. Do this several times until the dough is smooth and elastic.

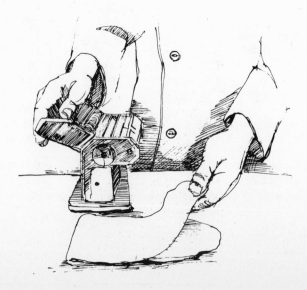

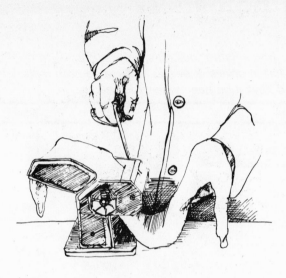

3. Pass the dough through the rollers at progressively narrower settings until it is the thickness you prefer. You will have to cut the dough in half occasionally as the dough becomes too long to handle.

4. Now pass the strips of dough through the slicing rollers — spaghetti, fettucine, or the more fancy shapes if your machine produces them.

Pasta al Sugo

Pasta al sugo is pasta which is first cooked in boiling water, and then served or tossed with a sauce. Here are some of the most popular shapes.

Spaghetti. This is the most famous of all pasta shapes, and goes with many different sauces. Its long, round rods come in varying thicknesses, and you must choose your favorites.

Spaghettini. This is very thin spaghetti.

Vermicelli. "Little worms". These are thin spaghetti strands, and very delicate.

Linguine. "Little tongues". This is flat spaghetti, but very narrow – so it goes well with many sauces, including creamed ones.

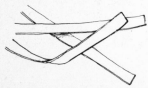

Fettucine. "Little ribbons". These noodles are flat, and about 1/4" wide. One of the most popular of all noodles, they can be served with meat sauce, go beautifully with creamed sauces, and are also very easy to make at home.

Tagliatelle. This noodle is similar to fettucine, and in fact, fettucine is just the Roman name for tagliatelle. It comes in different widths, and is good with all kinds of sauces.

Salsa Bolognese

Meat Sauce

This sauce is not only delicious on spaghetti, but is also used in many other Italian dishes. It freezes well, so you can make lots at one time and have it on hand when you need it.

Ingredients	Regular	Metric
Olive oil	2 tbsp.	30 ml
Onion, chopped	1	1
Garlic cloves, minced	2	2
Celery stalk, diced	1	1
Carrot, diced	1	1
Ground beef	1 lb.	500 g
Bay leaves, crumbled	2	2
Nutmeg	Pinch	Pinch
Basil	1/4 tsp.	1 ml
Salt	1/2 tsp.	2 ml
Pepper	Pinch	Pinch
Tomato paste	10 oz.	300 ml
Tomatoes, peeled and chopped	3 cups	750 ml
Red wine	4 oz.	125 ml
Beef stock	4 oz.	125 ml

1. Heat the oil in a large frying pan and cook the onion, garlic, celery and carrot for 5 minutes.
2. Add meat and cook, stirring until it is browned.
3. Add the next 9 ingredients and simmer for 1 hour.

Serves 4-6

Salsa di Pomodoro

Tomato Sauce

Tomato sauce is the basic ingredient in many Italian recipes, so it makes sense to make a lot at one time when your garden tomatoes are ripe, and freeze the extra sauce for the winter months.

Ingredients	Regular	Metric
Olive oil	4 oz.	125 ml
Onion, chopped	1	1
Garlic cloves, chopped	2	2
Basil, chopped	1 tbsp.	15 ml
Nutmeg	1/2 tsp.	2 ml
Sugar	2 tbsp.	30 ml
Salt	1 tsp.	5 ml
Pepper	1/2 tsp.	2 ml
Plum tomatoes, peeled	4 lbs.	2 kg
Tomato paste	10 oz.	300 ml
Red wine	4 oz.	125 ml
Butter	2 tbsp.	30 ml

1. Heat oil in a large pot and cook onion, garlic and seasonings for 5 minutes.
2. Mash tomatoes up, removing any hard parts, and add to the pot with the tomato paste, wine and butter. Simmer for 30 minutes, stirring often. When the sauce is fairly thick, and the golden oil floats on top, the sauce is done.

Serves 8-10

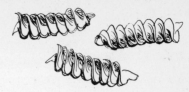

Rotini. "Turrets". These unusual pasta shapes are excellent at holding any kind of pasta sauce.

Rigatoni. Large, ribbed "elbow" macaroni, good with many sauces.

Pennine Rigate. Large pasta tubes with diagonally cut ends. Serve with any sauce.

Ziti. "Bridegrooms". These are large macaroni tubes about 3" wide. Variations are ziti rigati, "grooved bridegrooms", and zitoni, "husky bridegrooms". Take your choice.

Galle. "Bow ties". A decorative shape which will make any pasta dish special.

► *Pesto, the classic uncooked sauce of basil and garlic, is a specialty of Genoa, and as its name suggests, should have the consistency of a creamy paste. Toss it with the pasta right at the table, so everyone can get the benefit of the aroma and the beautiful green color.*

► *You can easily make a lot of pesto sauce when fresh basil is readily available in the summer, and freeze it for use all year long. Just omit the butter and cheeses when you're blending the sauce, then put the mixture in airtight containers and place them in the freezer. Before using, thaw in the refrigerator. Add the butter and cheeses just before serving for a really fresh taste.*

► *If pasta is going to be used with an anchovy sauce, don't put any salt into the cooking water.*

Salsa alla Genovese

Pesto Sauce

As the name suggests, this famous sauce from Genoa should be like a paste. Traditionally, it was made with a mortar and pestle, but nowadays a blender does a good job with a lot less effort.

Ingredients	Regular	Metric
Fresh basil leaves	1 cup	250 ml
Pine nuts	4 oz.	125 ml
Garlic cloves, peeled	2	2
Olive oil	1 cup	250 ml
Soft butter	6 tbsp.	90 ml
Salt	1/2 tsp.	2 ml
Pepper	Pinch	Pinch
Romano cheese, grated	1 cup	250 ml
Parmesan cheese, grated	1 cup	250 ml

1. Wash and drain the basil leaves, then place in a blender with the pine nuts, garlic and half the oil. Blend for 1 minute.
2. Add butter, salt and pepper, and blend again while adding the rest of the oil slowly until mixture has a paste-like consistency. Mix in the cheeses thoroughly.

Serves 4-6

Spaghetti con Acciughe

Spaghetti with Anchovy Sauce

This is a well-known dish from Southern Italy. It features anchovies, so shouldn't need any extra salt.

Ingredients	Regular	Metric
Olive oil	4 tbsp.	60 ml
Onion, chopped	1	1
Garlic clove, chopped	1	1
Pitted black olives, chopped	12	12
Capers	1 tbsp.	15 ml
Anchovy fillets, chopped	8	8
Basil	Pinch	Pinch
Pepper	Pinch	Pinch

Tomatoes, peeled and chopped	4	4
Tomato paste	2 tbsp.	30 ml
Red wine	4 oz.	125 ml
Spaghetti, cooked and drained	1 lb.	500 g
Parmesan cheese, grated	4 oz.	125 ml

1. Heat the oil in a frying pan and cook the onion and garlic for 5 minutes.
2. Add next 8 ingredients and simmer for 10-15 minutes, then adjust seasonings.
3. Put cooked pasta on a heated plate and pour sauce on top. Top with grated cheese and serve at once.

Serves 4

Linguine con Vongole in Bianco

Linguine with White Clam Sauce

This beautiful dish is a classic. Linguine is dressed lightly and delicately with a sauce of butter, clams, and wine. A fine sprinkling of cheese and parsley adds extra color and flavor.

Ingredients	Regular	Metric
Butter	4 tbsp.	60 ml
Garlic cloves, minced	2	2
Onion, chopped	1/2	1/2
Baby clams, chopped	10 oz. can	300 ml
White wine	2 oz.	50 ml
Clam juice from can	2 oz.	50 ml
Parsley, chopped	2 tbsp.	30 ml
Linguine, cooked and drained	1 lb.	500 g
Parmesan cheese, grated	4 oz.	125 ml

1. Melt the butter in a large frying pan and cook the garlic and onion for 5 minutes.
2. Add the clams, wine, and clam juice, and simmer for 10 minutes.
3. Add the parsley and cooked pasta. Toss well.
4. Place on a heated platter and top with grated cheese before serving.

Serves 4-6

Anchovy/Acciughe

Anchovies are small fish of the herring family, found and used widely in the Mediterranean. They are caught only when the moon is waning, and in Italy they are served fresh — either fried or grilled. Sometimes only tinned anchovies are available, but they are still delicious used in salads, as a garnish on pizza, or even eaten with toast and bread.

If the anchovies have been packed in salt instead of oil, they are called *alici* or *sardelle* and should be soaked in water for awhile before cooking.

"Pasta is the food of fantasy. It's at home with almost any other food or any sauce, so use your imagination and cook a pasta dish without using a recipe sometimes."

Tomato/Pomodoro

Although the most popular tomatoes in North America are the round red variety, for cooking and making sauces the very best are the Italian plum tomatoes. They're meaty and firm, and make a sauce which is thick enough to stick to the pasta.

In the summer they can be bought or grown fresh, but canned ones are fine to use all year long. Scoop the seeds out before using with your thumb or a small spoon.

Basil and tomatoes make one of the greatest pairs of complementary tastes in cooking, but other ingredients go well with tomatoes too — oregano, thyme, parsley, chives, salt and sugar are some.

Fettucine con Frutti di Mare

Fettucine with Seafood Sauce

"Frutti di mare" means a collection of shellfish or seafood. Italy's long coastline on the Mediterranean and Adriatic makes this dish popular in many regions.

Ingredients	Regular	Metric
Oil	4 tbsp.	60 ml
Butter	2 tbsp.	30 ml
Onion, sliced thin	1	1
Garlic clove, chopped	1	1
Crab or lobster meat	4 oz.	125 g
Baby shrimp	4 oz.	125 g
Cuttlefish or squid, cooked and sliced	4 oz.	125 g
Baby clams, cooked	12	12
Tomato, peeled and chopped	1	1
Tomato paste	2 tbsp.	30 ml
White wine	4 oz.	125 ml
Salt	1/2 tsp.	2 ml
Pepper	Pinch	Pinch
Fettucine, cooked and drained	1 lb.	500 g
Parsley, chopped	2 tbsp.	30 ml
Parmesan cheese, grated	2 tbsp.	30 ml
Chili peppers	Pinch	Pinch

1. Heat oil and butter in a frying pan and cook onion and garlic for 5 minutes.
2. Add fish and cook 5 minutes.
3. Add tomato, tomato paste, wine, salt, and pepper, and simmer 12 minutes.
4. Toss sauce with cooked fettucine, and serve with parsley, grated cheese and chili peppers on top.

Serves 4-6

Rigatoni con Aragosta

Rigatoni with Lobster Sauce

This large pasta has a nice bite, and is good with all kinds of chunky sauces—especially this one, made with lobster and tomatoes.

Ingredients	Regular	Metric
Olive oil	2 tbsp.	30 ml
Butter	2 tbsp.	30 ml
Onion, sliced thinly	1	1
Garlic cloves, chopped	2	2
Celery stalk, sliced thinly	2	2
Carrot, shredded	1	1
Tomato paste	2 tbsp.	30 ml
Tomatoes, peeled and chopped	1 cup	250 ml
Sherry or vermouth	2 oz.	50 ml
Chicken or fish stock	6 oz.	200 ml
Chili peppers	1 tsp.	5 ml
Salt	1/2 tsp.	2 ml
Pepper	Pinch	Pinch
Cooked lobster meat, chopped	12 oz.	375 g
Rigatoni, cooked and drained	1 lb.	500 g
Parmesan, grated	2 oz.	50 ml
Parsley, chopped	1 tbsp.	5 ml

1. Heat oil and butter in a large frying pan, and cook onion, garlic, celery and carrot for 5 minutes.
2. Add the tomato paste, tomatoes, liquids and seasonings. Simmer for 15 minutes.
3. Add lobster and cook 5-7 minutes.
4. Place cooked pasta on heated platter and cover with sauce. Sprinkle with grated cheese and parsley, and serve immediately.

Serves 4-6

"The ingredients in a sauce should be the same as partners in a good marriage. They should be wonderful joined together, but still themselves. A tomato should taste like a tomato, and a green pepper should taste like a green pepper. Don't cook the sauce to death so that you can't tell the difference."

Garlic/Aglio

Garlic, a member of the onion family, has been popular since the beginning of recorded time as a seasoning and a medicine. The Chinese, Egyptians and Greeks all used it, although the law in Ancient Greece forbade anyone who had eaten garlic to go inside the temple of Cybele.

Down through the years, garlic has been used to prevent illness and in the Middle Ages was even thought to be a cure for leprosy. Worn around the neck, it is said to ward off evil, and vampires are supposed to find it particularly loathsome.

Today, garlic is widely accepted as a necessary flavoring in sauces, stews and salads, and is one of the most important staples in Italian cooking.

How to Buy. Garlic comes in a head or bulb made up of separate cloves. Look for heads which are sold loose in a bin, so you can choose the ones you want. They should be firm and crisp – squeeze first to test for any softness. Avoid heads with brown spots, split skins, yellowing cloves or green sprouts.

Bocconcini alla Panna

Bocconcini with Cream Sauce

Medium-sized ribbed macaroni tossed with a cream sauce containing mushrooms, ham and walnuts.

Ingredients	Regular	Metric
Butter	2 tbsp.	30 ml
Oil	2 tbsp.	30 ml
Mushrooms, sliced	8	8
Red pepper, cored and sliced	1	1
Prosciutto or ham, chopped	4 oz.	125 ml
Heavy cream	8 oz.	250 ml
White wine	2 oz.	50 ml
Chicken stock	2 oz.	50 ml
Walnuts, chopped finely	2 oz.	50 ml
Nutmeg	Pinch	Pinch
Tabasco sauce	4 drops	4 drops
Salt	1/2 tsp.	2 ml
Bocconcini, cooked and drained	1 lb.	500 g
Parmesan cheese, grated	4 oz.	125 ml
Parsley, chopped	2 tbsp.	30 ml

1. Heat butter and oil in a frying pan and cook mushrooms, red pepper and ham for 5 minutes.
2. Add cream, wine, stock, walnuts and seasonings. Simmer for 10 minutes.
3. Toss sauce with cooked pasta, and serve topped with grated cheese and parsley.

Serves 4-6

Perciatelli Calabrese

Perciatelli Calabrese Style

In Southern Italy, we like our sauces a little spicier. Try this sauce from Calabria—you'll love it.

Ingredients	Regular	Metric
Olive oil	2 tbsp.	30 ml
Italian sausage, sliced	2	2

	Regular	Metric
Garlic clove, chopped	1	1
Carrot, peeled and sliced	1	1
Green pepper, chopped	1	1
Red pepper, chopped	1	1
Chili peppers	1/4 tsp.	1 ml
Chicken stock	2 oz.	50 ml
Bolognese sauce	2 cups	500 ml
Perciatelli, cooked and drained	1 lb.	500 g
Parmesan cheese, grated	4 oz.	125 ml

1. Heat the oil in a large pot and cook the sausage, garlic, carrot, green pepper and chili peppers for 5 minutes, until the sausage is cooked through.
2. Add chicken stock and simmer for 5 minutes.
3. Add the meat sauce and simmer another 10 minutes, then pour over cooked pasta and top with cheese.

Serves 4-6

Bocconcini alla Ricotta

Bocconcini with Ricotta

The ribs in this medium-sized macaroni are excellent for catching this sauce of butter, tomato, and ricotta cheese.

Ingredients	Regular	Metric
Butter	4 oz.	125 ml
Green onions, chopped	2	2
Green pepper, chopped	1	1
Tomato, chopped	1	1
Ricotta cheese	2 cups	500 ml
Parmesan cheese, grated	4 tbsp.	60 ml
Wine	2 oz.	50 ml
Parsley, chopped	2 tbsp.	30 ml
Bocconcini, cooked and drained	1 lb.	500 g

1. Heat butter in a frying pan and cook onions, green pepper, and tomato for 5 minutes.
2. Add cheeses, wine and parsley, and cook another 5 minutes over low heat.
3. Toss with cooked pasta and serve with extra grated cheese if desired.

Serves 4-6

How to Store. The fresher the garlic, the sweeter the taste, so the best idea is to buy garlic as you need it, although it will keep for up to ten days if stored properly.

Keep at room temperature in an uncovered jar or aerated plastic container. Department stores and specialty shops now sell ceramic garlic holders with plenty of holes to let the air circulate, and these are very good and attractive. Never keep garlic in the refrigerator or it will sprout and even mildew.

How to Use. The best way to prepare for use in sauces or sauté, is to peel the individual cloves and mince them by hand. Smash the peeled clove flat with the side of a large knife, then mince into even pieces. Cook gently, and never let the garlic brown as this will make the oil bitter and spoil the taste of the dish.

Slivered, the cloves can be inserted into meat to impart a delicate flavor while it is roasting, then removed just before serving. This is particularly effective with lamb.

A garlic clove can enhance salads if it is bruised and rubbed around the salad bowl before the greens are added.

▶ *When cooking garlic for a sauce, never let it brown in the oil as this will make it bitter.*

Tagliatellini alle Vongole in Rosso

Egg Noodles with Red Clam Sauce

Tagliatellini is like spaghetti, but more delicate. It has a different bite and goes well with all sauces, including this one.

Ingredients	Regular	Metric
Olive oil	2 tbsp.	30 ml
Garlic cloves, minced	2	2
Onion, chopped	1	1
Baby clams, chopped	10 oz. can	300 ml
Clam juice from can	2 oz.	50 ml
Marjoram	Pinch	Pinch
Basil	1/2 tsp.	2 ml
Tomato paste	1 tbsp.	15 ml
Tomatoes, peeled and chopped	2	2
Pepper	Pinch	Pinch
Tagliatellini, cooked and drained	1 lb.	500 g
Parmesan cheese, grated	4 oz.	125 ml

1. Heat the oil in a frying pan and cook the garlic and onion for 5 minutes.
2. Add the chopped clams, clam juice, seasonings, tomato paste and tomatoes. Sprinkle with pepper and simmer for 10-15 minutes.
3. Add the cooked pasta and toss well. Serve immediately with grated cheese on top.

Serves 4-6

Fettucine alla Panna

Fettucine with Cream Sauce

This dish is also called "Fettucine Alfredo" because it became popular at Alfredo's Restaurant in Rome.

Ingredients	Regular	Metric
Fettucine, cooked and drained	1 lb.	500 g
Butter	4 tbsp.	60 ml
Egg yolks, beaten	2	2

➤ *If a sauce contains eggs, never let it come to a boil unless flour has also been added, or the eggs will curdle.*

Heavy cream	4 oz.	125 ml
Parmesan cheese, grated	4 oz.	125 ml
Salt	1/2 tsp.	2 ml
Pepper	Pinch	Pinch

1. Add butter to cooked, drained pasta. Toss until butter is melted, then add other ingredients and toss again.
2. Serve immediately, passing a bowl of grated cheese and a peppermill.

Serves 4-6

➤ *Always try to use whipping cream in sauces, as lighter cream has a tendency to curdle when added to other ingredients, (especially oil and butter) because of its lower fat content.*

Vermicelli con Funghi

Vermicelli with Mushrooms

A light and creamy sauce of ham and mushrooms, tossed with vermicelli—the most delicate of all the pastas.

Ingredients	Regular	Metric
Butter	4 tbsp.	60 ml
Ham or prosciutto, chopped	4 oz.	125 ml
Mushrooms, sliced	8	8
Tomato, peeled and chopped	1	1
Pepper	Pinch	Pinch
Egg yolks, beaten	2	2
Heavy cream	6 oz.	200 ml
Basil	1/4 tsp.	1 ml
Vermicelli, cooked and drained	1 lb.	500 g
Parmesan cheese, grated	4 oz.	125 ml

1. Heat butter in a large pot and cook the ham, mushrooms, tomato and pepper for 5 minutes.
2. Mix the egg yolks, cream and basil together in a bowl.
3. Put cooked pasta in the pot with the ham and mushrooms and toss well.
4. Take off the heat, and add cream and egg mixture. Toss until thick and well-coated. Serve immediately with grated cheese.

Serves 4-6

Porcini Mushrooms

Porcini are Italian mushrooms much prized by gourmets and good cooks everywhere. They are available dried in Italian markets and many specialty shops, and are valued primarily for the unique taste they impart to any dish which calls for mushrooms. Because they are dried, they must be reconstituted by soaking before being used.

Place the mushrooms in warm water and leave for twenty minutes, then remove, but don't throw away the delicious soaking water. Instead, pass it through a sieve lined with a paper towel to remove any grit or sand, and use in the recipe for extra taste.

Spaghetti alla Caruso

Spaghetti with Whiskey and Chicken Livers

Chicken livers and whiskey make this dish unique, and almost as famous as the Italian tenor it was named after.

Ingredients	Regular	Metric
Olive oil	2 tbsp.	30 ml
Garlic cloves, chopped	3	3
Onion, chopped	1	1
Anchovies, chopped	6	6
Mushrooms, sliced	8	8
Chicken livers, sliced	8	8
Green pepper, chopped	1	1
Nutmeg	Pinch	Pinch
Chili peppers	Pinch	Pinch
Basil	1/2 tsp.	2 ml
Red wine	4 oz.	125 ml
Tomatoes, drained	14 oz. can	450 ml
Tomato paste	4 tbsp.	60 ml
Whiskey	4 oz.	125 ml
Butter	1 tbsp.	15 ml
Salt	1/2 tsp.	2 ml
Pepper	Pinch	Pinch

Tomato Sauce

Here is an easy way to preserve tomatoes from your garden for later use.

First, peel the tomatoes by plunging them into boiling water and then cold water, and pulling off the skins. Then cut them in quarters, and scoop out the seeds with your fingers.

Put 4 pounds (about 30 medium tomatoes), 2 tablespoons of salt, 6 oz. of olive oil, and 8 leaves of fresh basil in a large pot.

Bring to a boil, and cook until there is no more froth on top, then pour into preserving jars, the kind with rubber rings, and store upside down until ready to use.

| Spaghetti, cooked and drained | 1 lb. | 500 g |
| Parmesan cheese, grated | 4 oz. | 125 ml |

1. Heat the oil in a large pot and cook the next 6 ingredients for 5 minutes. Add the next 10 ingredients and simmer for 10-15 minutes.
2. Place cooked pasta on a heated platter and pour sauce on top.
3. Sprinkle with grated cheese and serve immediately.

Serves 4-6

► *Never add salt, chili peppers, or any spice directly to a recipe in case of an accident. Measure the seasoning into the palm of your hand first.*

Paglia e Fieno

White and Green Pasta with Cream Sauce

This easy dish is delicious and lovely looking. The name means "straw and hay" because of the way the white and green pastas are intertwined and tossed up together. Try other types of thin pasta as well.

Ingredients	Regular	Metric
Butter	2 tbsp.	30 ml
Garlic clove, chopped	1	1
Mushrooms, sliced	8	8
Heavy cream	6 oz.	200 ml
Egg, beaten	1	1
Parmesan cheese, grated	4 oz.	125 ml
Nutmeg	Pinch	Pinch
Basil	1/4 tsp.	1 ml
Salt	1/2 tsp.	2 ml
Pepper	Pinch	Pinch
Green tagliatelli	8 oz.	250 g
White tagliatelli	8 oz.	250 g

1. Heat the butter in a large frying pan and cook the garlic and mushrooms for 5 minutes.
2. In a bowl, mix together the cream, egg, cheese and seasonings, and set aside.
3. Cook the green and white pasta separately and drain. Add to the frying pan and toss with the mushrooms.
4. Add the cream mixture and toss until sauce begins to thicken. Serve immediately with grated cheese.

Serves 4-6

Gorgonzola

Gorgonzola is a popular Italian blue cheese which was apparently invented by accident. Once, a wine store owner was given cheeses instead of money for payment – he put them down in the cellar and forgot all about them. When he finally discovered them, they had ripened beautifully, and with their creamy-white texture, and delicious green-blue mold running through, they rapidly became famous. Gorgonzola is usually eaten sliced, crumbled for soups and salad dressings, and sometimes in recipes.

Maccaroncelli con Gorgonzola

Macaroni with Gorgonzola Cheese

Gorgonzola is a blue-veined cheese similar to roquefort, but sweeter and milder. It still has plenty of bite though, so don't use too much.

Ingredients	Regular	Metric
Butter	4 tbsp.	60 ml
Onion, chopped	1	1
Celery stalk, chopped	1	1
Green pepper, diced	1/2	1/2
Tomato, peeled and chopped	1	1
Gorgonzola cheese, diced	4 oz.	125 ml
White wine	4 oz.	125 ml
Romano cheese, grated	2 tbsp.	30 ml
Maccaroncelli, cooked and drained	1 lb.	500 g

1. Melt the butter in a frying pan and cook the onion, celery and green pepper for 5 minutes.
2. Add tomato and cook for another few minutes, then add the gorgonzola.
3. When the cheese has melted, add the liquid and grated cheese. Simmer 5 minutes.
4. Toss with cooked pasta and serve immediately.

Serves 4-6

Spaghetti alla Carbonara

Spaghetti with Crushed Peppers

This very popular dish got its name because the little pieces of crushed peppercorns sprinkled on top look like bits of charcoal, or "carbonara".

Ingredients	Regular	Metric
Butter	2 tbsp.	30 ml
Oil	2 tbsp.	30 ml
Bacon, chopped	4 oz.	125 ml
Spaghetti, cooked and drained	1 lb.	500 g

Salt	1/2 tsp.	2 ml
Pepper	Pinch	Pinch
Eggs	2	2
White wine	2 oz.	50 ml
Parmesan cheese, grated	2 oz.	50 ml
Romano cheese, grated	2 oz.	50 ml
Nutmeg	Pinch	Pinch
Peppercorns, crushed	1 tbsp.	15 ml

1. Heat the butter and oil in a large pot and cook the bacon for 5 minutes.
2. Add cooked pasta, season with salt and pepper, and toss.
3. In a bowl, lightly beat the eggs with the wine, cheeses and nutmeg.
4. Take the pasta off the heat and pour in the egg mixture, then toss for a few minutes.
5. Place on a heated platter, top with crushed peppercorns, and serve.

Serves 4-6

Pepper/Pepe Nero

The peppercorn is the world's most widely used spice. Not only does freshly ground black pepper add a savory quality to practically every kind of food, it is also used in the making of sausages, in pickling and marinating liquids, and as a tasty tenderizer in dishes like pepper steak. Whole black peppercorns, crushed, are the most important ingredient in spaghetti carbonara.

► *Never try to make pasta dough in damp or humid weather.*

Ziti con Maiale Misto

Ziti with Mixed Pork Sauce

Small tubes of pasta tossed with a sauce of mixed pork and tomatoes.

Ingredients	Regular	Metric
Olive oil	2 oz.	50 ml
Onion, sliced	1	1
Garlic cloves, minced	2	2
Cooked pork, chopped	2 oz.	50 ml
Capocollo, chopped	2 oz.	50 ml
Bacon or pancetta, chopped	2 oz.	50 ml
Sweet red pepper, chopped	1	1
Red wine	4 oz.	125 ml
Beef stock	4 oz.	125 ml
Tomatoes, peeled and chopped	2	2
Tomato paste	2 tbsp.	30 ml
Basil	1/4 tsp.	1 ml
Salt	1/2 tsp.	2 ml
Pepper	Pinch	Pinch
Ziti, cooked and drained	1 lb.	500 g
Parmesan cheese, grated	4 oz.	125 ml

1. Heat the oil in a large frying pan and cook the onion, garlic and meat for 5 minutes.
2. Add the next 8 ingredients and simmer for 15 minutes.
3. Toss the cooked pasta with the sauce and serve with grated cheese on top.

Serves 4-6

"La salsa e indispenzabile per la buona cucina. The sauce is indispensable to a good kitchen."

▶ *When the hard kernels of Durham wheat are ground up, they produce a hard, fine-grained substance called semolina. Always be sure the pasta or flour you buy has the names "Durham" or "semolina" wheat on the package, because its superior quality lets the pasta keep its shape and "bite".*

Rigatoni alla Vodka

Rigatoni with Vodka Sauce

Start with double the amount of vodka called for. Use half in the recipe, and drink the rest in a toast to this beautiful dish!

Ingredients	Regular	Metric
Olive oil	2 oz.	500 ml
Butter	2 tbsp.	30 ml
Onion, chopped	1	1
Garlic cloves, chopped	2	2
Tomatoes, peeled and chopped	1 cup	250 ml
Ham or prosciutto, chopped	4 oz.	125 ml
Heavy cream	6 oz.	200 ml
Red wine	4 oz.	125 ml
Vodka	2 oz.	50 ml
Parmesan cheese, grated	2 tbsp.	30 ml
Romano cheese, grated	2 tbsp.	30 ml
Salt	1/2 tsp.	2 ml
Pepper	Pinch	Pinch
Rigatoni, cooked and drained	1 lb.	500 g
Parsley, chopped	2 tbsp.	30 ml
Chili peppers	1 tsp.	5 ml

1. Heat oil and butter in a frying pan, and cook onion and garlic for 5 minutes.
2. Add tomatoes and ham, then simmer for 10 minutes.
3. Add cream, wine, vodka, cheeses, salt and pepper, and reduce over medium heat for several minutes.
4. Toss with cooked pasta, and serve with parsley and chili peppers sprinkled on top.

Serves 4-6

Romano

Romano cheese is hard and sharp-flavored, very much like parmesan. It is a fine grating cheese, and is most often used on pasta.

Rotini con Zucchini

Rotini with Zucchini

Rotini has an elegant corkscrew shape which is excellent for catching the sauce.

> ▶ *When storing hard cheese after cutting or grating, put butter or oil on the cut edges before wrapping in foil and putting in the refrigerator. This will seal the edges and keep the cheese from drying out.*

Ingredients	Regular	Metric
Oil	2 tbsp.	30 ml
Butter	2 tbsp.	30 ml
Onion, sliced thinly	1	1
Garlic clove, chopped	1	1
Prosciutto or ham, chopped	4 oz.	125 ml
Zucchini	2	2
Chicken stock	1 cup	250 ml
Salt	1/2 tsp.	2 ml
Peppercorns, crushed	1/2 tsp.	2 ml
Sugar	1/2 tsp.	2 ml
Basil	1/2 tsp.	2 ml
Chili peppers	1/2 tsp.	2 ml
Rotini, cooked and drained	1 lb.	500 g
Parmesan cheese, grated	4 tbsp.	60 ml

1. Heat oil and butter in a frying pan, and cook onion and garlic for 5 minutes. Add ham and cook for 3 minutes more.
2. Slice zucchini and cut into match sticks, then add to pan and cook for 5-7 minutes.
3. Add stock and seasonings, and simmer for 10 minutes.
4. Toss with cooked pasta, and sprinkle with grated cheese before serving.

Serves 4-6

Spaghettini con Polpettini

Thin Spaghetti with Small Meatballs

This might seem to be a dish for weight-watchers because it is thin and small. But it is very good, so don't wait—just watch out!

Ingredients	Regular	Metric
Ground beef	1 lb.	500 g
Breadcrumbs	2 oz.	50 ml
Salt	1/2 tsp.	2 ml
Pepper	Pinch	Pinch
Nutmeg	1/4 tsp.	1 ml
Chili powder	1/4 tsp.	1 ml
Oil	2 oz.	50 ml
Onion, chopped	1	1
Garlic clove, chopped	1	1
Tomatoes, peeled and chopped	2 cups	500 ml
Chicken stock	6 oz.	200 ml
Red wine	2 oz.	50 ml
Tomato paste	2 tbsp.	30 ml
Spaghettini, cooked and drained	1 lb.	500 g
Parmesan cheese, grated	4 oz.	125 ml

1. Combine ground beef, breadcrumbs, salt, pepper, nutmeg and chili powder, then form the mixture into small balls with the palms of your hands.
2. Heat oil in frying pan, and cook onion and garlic for 5 minutes.
3. Add meatballs and brown all over.
4. Add tomatoes, stock, wine and tomato paste, and simmer for 30 minutes.
5. Place cooked pasta on a heated platter. Season sauce to taste with salt and pepper and pour over the pasta. Sprinkle with grated cheese and serve immediately.

Serves 4-6

► *To ripen tomatoes, put them in a paper bag with a small, ripe apple, then punch some air-holes in the sides of the bag to let out the carbon dioxide. The apple will quicken the ripening. When the tomatoes are soft, store them in the refrigerator for up to two days.*

Fettucine Verde del Capitano

Green Fettucine with Smoked Salmon

Green pasta contrasts colorfully with the red salmon and the white parmesan cheese. An intriguing and beautiful combination of ingredients.

Ingredients	Regular	Metric
Oil	2 tbsp.	30 ml
Butter	2 tbsp.	30 ml
Green onions, chopped	2	2
Smoked salmon, chopped	4 oz.	125 g
White wine	4 oz.	125 ml
Chicken stock	4 oz.	125 ml
Heavy cream	6 oz.	200 ml
Nutmeg	1/4 tsp.	1 ml
Cayenne	Pinch	Pinch
Green fettucine, cooked and drained	1 lb.	500 g
Parsley, chopped	1 tbsp.	15 ml
Parmesan cheese, grated	4 oz.	125 ml

1. Heat oil and butter in a large frying pan, and cook onions for 5 minutes.
2. Add the smoked salmon and cook for a few minutes more, then stir in liquids and seasonings, and cook until sauce has reduced by half.
3. Toss with cooked pasta, then top with parsley and grated cheese.

Serves 4-6

Linguine alla Rustica

Linguine with Spinach and Walnuts

Pasta is covered with a spinach and walnut sauce—an unusual but delicious combination.

Ingredients	Regular	Metric
Olive oil	2 tbsp.	30 ml
Garlic cloves, chopped	2	2
Bacon slices, diced	3	3

➤ *It is much better to chop or slice onions by hand as mechanical methods make them too mushy.*

Green onions, chopped	2	2
White wine	4 oz.	125 ml
Chili peppers	Pinch	Pinch
Walnuts, chopped	4 oz.	125 ml
Spinach, cooked and chopped	10 oz.	300 ml
Butter	2 tbsp.	30 ml
Salt	1/2 tsp.	2 ml
Pepper	1/8 tsp.	1/2 ml
Linguine, cooked and drained	1 lb.	500 g
Parmesan cheese, grated	4 oz.	125 ml

1. Heat oil in a large frying pan and cook garlic and bacon until bacon is crisp. Add green onion and cook 3 minutes more.
2. Stir in wine, chili peppers, nuts, spinach and butter. Season with salt and pepper and cook for 5 minutes.
3. Pour sauce over cooked pasta and top with grated cheese.

Serves 4-6

➤ *After chopping onions or garlic, rinse your hands in a little vinegar, then wash them thoroughly in hot soapy water to eliminate the strong clinging odors from your fingers.*

Spaghetti all' Amatriciana

Spaghetti with Bacon and Tomatoes

This Roman recipe gets its name from the little town of Amatrice, which is located in the hills just outside the city.

Ingredients	Regular	Metric
Olive oil	2 tbsp.	30 ml
Onion, sliced thinly	1	1
Lean bacon, diced	4 oz.	125 ml
White wine	4 oz.	125 ml
Tomatoes, peeled and chopped	2	2
Salt	1/2 tsp.	2 ml
Pepper	Pinch	Pinch
Spaghetti, cooked and drained	1 lb.	500 g
Parmesan cheese, grated	2 oz.	50 ml

1. Heat the oil in a frying pan and cook the onions for 5 minutes.
2. Add the bacon and cook for 3 minutes, then pour in the wine and continue to cook for a few minutes more.
3. Add tomatoes and seasonings, and simmer for 15 minutes.
4. Place cooked pasta on a heated platter and pour sauce on top. Sprinkle with grated cheese and serve immediately.

Serves 4-6

➤ *To cut down on tears, partially freeze onions before peeling and chopping them.*

► *Chewing a sprig of parsley after a meal will eliminate the smell of garlic, and make the breath fresh and sweet.*

Lumache con Granchio Dimare

Lumache with Crab Meat Sauce

Large shells of pasta compliment this sauce made from crab—the king of shellfish.

Ingredients	Regular	Metric
Oil	2 tbsp.	30 ml
Onion, chopped	1	1
Garlic cloves, chopped	2	2
Green pepper, sliced thinly	1	1
Tomatoes, peeled and chopped	1	1
Crab meat	8 oz.	250 g
Heavy cream	6 oz.	200 ml
Salt	1/2 tsp.	2 ml
Pepper	Pinch	Pinch
Lumache, cooked and drained	1 lb.	500 g
Parsley, chopped	2 tbsp.	300 ml
Parmesan cheese, grated	2 tbsp.	30 ml

1. Heat oil in a frying pan and cook onion, garlic and green pepper for 5 minutes, then add tomato and cook for a few minutes more.
2. Add crab meat, cream, salt and pepper, and cook for 10 minutes.
3. Toss with cooked pasta, sprinkle with parsley and grated cheese and serve immediately.

Serves 4-6

Rigatoni con Pepperonata

Rigatoni with Hot Peppers

Large-ribbed elbow macaroni is perfect with this spicy sauce.

Ingredients	Regular	Metric
Olive oil	4 tbsp.	60 ml
Onion, thinly sliced	1	1
Hot red peppers, chopped	2	2
Garlic cloves, minced	2	2
Chili peppers	1/2 tsp.	2 ml
Tomato, peeled and chopped	1	1
Tomato paste	4 tbsp.	60 ml

► *Always wash your hands after adding a "pinch" of chili peppers or powder. Otherwise, the hot chili might get in your eyes and make you cry.*

Basil	1 tsp.	5 ml
White wine	4 oz.	125 ml
Salt	1/2 tsp.	2 ml
Pepper	Pinch	Pinch
Parsley, chopped	1 tsp.	15 ml
Rigatoni, cooked and drained	1 lb.	500 g
Parmesan cheese, grated	4 oz.	125 ml

1. Heat oil in a large frying pan and cook onion, peppers and garlic for 5 minutes.
2. Add chili peppers, tomato, tomato paste, basil and wine. Simmer for 10 minutes, then add salt, pepper and parsley, and cook 5 minutes more.
3. Place cooked pasta on a heated platter and pour sauce on top. Serve sprinkled with grated cheese.

Serves 4-6

Lasagne
Noodle Casserole

Everybody's favorite and a wonderful dish for a party. Make it meatless by substituting tomato sauce, or use green noodles for color.

Ingredients	Regular	Metric
Lasagne noodles	1 lb.	500 g
Bolognese sauce	4 cups	1 L
Ricotta cheese	8 oz.	250 g
Mozzarella cheese, grated	8 oz.	250 ml
Parmesan cheese, grated	4 oz.	125 ml
Bechamel sauce	1 cup	250 ml

1. Preheat oven to 350°F./180°C.
2. Cook and drain lasagne noodles, and rinse in cold water.
3. Oil a large baking dish and place some meat sauce on the bottom. Cover with a layer of noodles.
4. Mix the cheeses with the white sauce and put a layer on the noodles, and then more meat sauce.
5. Put more noodles on crossways and continue layering until you reach the top of the dish, ending with meat sauce.
6. Sprinkle with more grated cheese and cook for 30 minutes. Remove and let stand for several minutes, then cut into squares and serve.

Serves 8-10

Pasta al Forno

Pasta al forno is a method in which pasta shapes are cooked in boiling water, and then filled with a stuffing and baked with a sauce. The most popular are:

Lasagne. This extra wide noodle is flat, and sometimes curly at the edges. When it is made with spinach, it is called lasagne verde.

Cannelloni. "Big pipes". These are the largest of the stuffed pasta shapes, and are usually served two to a person.

Manicotti. "Little muff". A large ribbed tube, cut on a slant at both ends.

▶ *After lasagne has been taken out of the oven, always let it sit and set for about fifteen minutes. This way, everything will come together and be easier to cut into squares.*

1. Roll out the dough by hand or use the pasta machine, as the width of the roller, about 6 inches, is perfect for cannelloni.

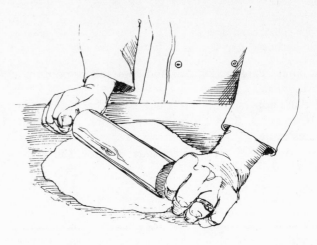

2. Cut the pasta into large squares, about 6 inches square. Shape the filling in the form of a sausage and place on each pasta square.

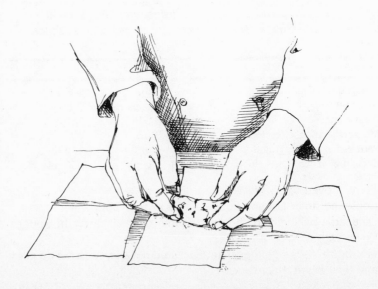

3. Roll up the pasta around the filling. Now place cannelloni in a baking dish.

Cannelloni alla Fiorentina

Cannelloni with Ricotta and Spinach

A dish which includes spinach is sometimes named "fiorentina" after the city of Florence. The spinach cooked with cheeses is a classic from this city and a delicious combination.

Ingredients	Regular	Metric
Spinach	8 oz.	250 g
Ricotta cheese	1 lb.	500 g
Parmesan cheese, grated	4 oz.	125 ml
Eggs	2	2
Salt	1/2 tsp.	2 ml
Pepper	Pinch	Pinch
Cannelloni, cooked and drained	10-12	10-12
Bechamel sauce	2 cups	500 ml

1. Preheat oven to 350°F/180°C.
2. Wash and cook spinach in its own water for 5 minutes. Drain well and chop finely.
3. Mix with cheeses, eggs, salt and pepper, and stuff the cooked cannelloni.
4. Place 1 cup of sauce in the bottom of a baking dish and lay cannelloni on top. Cover with remaining sauce and cook in the oven for 30 minutes.

Serves 4-6

▶ *Let finished pasta dough rest for thirty minutes before cutting. It will reduce the elasticity, and make the dough easier to work with.*

Cannelloni alla Napolitana

Cannelloni with Veal Stuffing

A combination of veal and sauces is made just a little different with the addition of shredded lettuce, which makes the stuffing lighter and more tender. Ground beef can be substituted for veal if you prefer.

Ingredients	Regular	Metric
Butter	2 tbsp.	30 ml
Ground veal	1 lb.	500 g
Salt	1/2 tsp.	2 ml
Pepper	Pinch	Pinch
Eggs	2	2
Iceberg lettuce, shredded	1 cup	250 ml
Romano cheese, grated	2 oz.	50 ml
Parsley, chopped	2 tbsp.	30 ml
Cannelloni, cooked and drained	12	12
Tomato sauce	1 cup	250 ml
Bechamel sauce	1 cup	250 ml
Parmesan cheese, grated	4 oz.	125 ml

1. Preheat the oven to 350°F./180°C.
2. Heat butter in a frying pan and cook meat until nicely browned, then mix with next 6 ingredients.
3. Stuff cooked cannelloni tubes with the meat mixture.
4. Spread half the tomato sauce in the bottom of a large cooking dish and lay the cannelloni on top. Add the remaining tomato sauce and pour the cream sauce on top.
5. Sprinkle the grated cheese over the sauces, then cook in the oven for 30 minutes.

Serves 4-6

▶ *Don't rinse pasta in cold water after it has cooked, because this spoils the texture and prevents the sauce from sticking. The only exception is if the pasta is to be added to a clear broth for soup, or used in "pasta al forno" where the pasta has to be handled before being put in the oven to bake.*

Ravioli con Formaggio

Ravioli with Cheese Stuffing

Tender squares of pasta stuffed with cheeses, and served with tomato sauce and grated parmesan. Ravioli are so good, they're worth the extra effort to make them.

Ingredients	Regular	Metric
Fresh pasta dough	2 lbs.	1 kg
Ricotta cheese	2 cups	250 ml
Parmesan cheese, grated	1 cup	125 ml
Onion, minced	1/2	1/2
Eggs	3	3
Salt	1/8 tsp.	1 ml
Pepper, freshly ground	1/8 tsp.	1 ml
Nutmeg	Pinch	Pinch
Tomato sauce	2 cups	250 ml

1. Make fresh pasta dough. Knead for 10 minutes until it is smooth and elastic, then cover and let rest for 30 minutes.
2. Mix together the ricotta, half the grated cheese, the onion, two of the eggs, and the seasonings.
3. Roll dough in pasta machine, or by hand, until you have strips the width of the machine—about 6"/15 cm—and as thin as leather. Don't make them too thin, though, otherwise the stuffing might break through.
4. Beat the remaining egg, and brush it over one strip of pasta, then put teaspoon-sized portions of stuffing on it, 2$^1/_2$"/6 cm apart.
5. Place another piece of rolled dough on top. Seal the edges and between the fillings with the heel of your hand, then cut into 2"/5 cm squares with a ravioli cutter.
6. When all the ravioli have been made, place in a large pot of boiling salted water, and cook at a gentle boil for 8-10 minutes or until the pastas float to the top.
7. Taste one to make sure they're done, then remove them to a heated platter with a slotted spoon. Cover with sauce, sprinkle the rest of the grated cheese on top and serve immediately.

Serves 4-6

Stuffing Variations

Ravioli with Meat Stuffing
  4 tbsp. oil
  2 cloves garlic, minced
  1 small onion, chopped
  8 oz. ground veal
  8 oz. ground beef
Heat the oil in a large frying pan and cook the garlic and onion for 5 minutes. Add the meats and cook and stir until browned, then drain and put into a large bowl with:
  Salt and pepper
  2 eggs
  2 tbsp. chopped parsley
  Pinch cinnamon
  1/2 cup breadcrumbs
If mixture is too dry, add a little white wine.

Ravioli with Ricotta and Spinach
This is made the same way as ravioli with cheese stuffing except that you add 1 pound of spinach.
Wash the leaves thoroughly, and remove any tough stems. Cook in a covered pan with no extra water for 5 minutes, then press out any excess moisture and chop finely.
Add to the cheese, then stuff and cook the ravioli in the usual way.

1. Roll out the dough by hand or use the pasta machine. Lay pasta sheets flat on the counter and brush with beaten egg.

2. Place small spoonfull-size balls of filling on the pasta sheet about every 2 inches. Now fold the other half of the pasta sheet over the top, or place another sheet over the top.

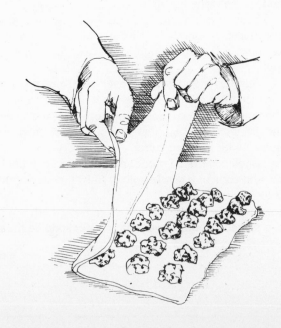

3. Seal the dough between the fillings by pressing down with the sides of your hand. Seal in a criss-cross pattern so that each filling is sealed in well.

4. Cut into individual ravioli with a cutter or knife by slicing where the seal was made. Don't cut too close to the filling or it will seep out during cooking.

Pizza

Historians say that pizza goes back to the Neolithic Age, but Neapolitans will swear that it originated in Naples with the arrival of the tomato in the 16th century. Although the Bourbons were pleased to offer it at their receptions in the Palace of Caserta, nowadays anyone can indulge in the infinite variety the pizza offers. It can be as simple as a tomato and cheese pizza, or have a vast number of ingredients on top. However it is served, it is one of the most popular snacks and finger dishes in the world, and a lot of fun to make at home.

Basic Pizza Dough

This recipe can be made ahead of time and frozen. You can roll it out and place on the pan before you freeze it if you like, which is very handy if you want to make "instant pizza" but you need a lot of freezer space for that.

Ingredients	Regular	Metric
Dry yeast	1 packet	1 packet
Warm water	2 cups	500 ml
Eggs	2	2
Sugar	2 tbsp.	30 ml
Oil	4 tbsp.	60 ml
Salt	1 tsp.	5 ml
Flour	4 cups	1 L

1. Put the yeast in warm water and stir until thoroughly dissolved, then let sit for five minutes.
2. Put into a large bowl with the eggs, sugar, oil and salt, and whisk until the mixture foams.
3. Add 3 cups of flour and stir until all the liquid has been absorbed, then work the rest of the flour in gradually with your hands until dough is soft and smooth and doesn't stick to the bowl.
4. Divide into 4 sections and shape each section into a patty. Put on a floured surface, cover with a towel, and let rise for 1 hour.
5. Roll each patty out to fit a 12"/30 cm round oiled pizza pan. Place dough on pan, pushing it out to fit with your fingertips. Make a lip around the edge by squeezing the dough between your thumb and fingers. Use immediately, or freeze for use later.

Makes 4-12"/30 cm rounds

Pizza Napolitana

Pizza with Cheese and Anchovies

Naples is the accepted home of the pizza, although historians say its origins go back thousands of years. This version is as close as you can get to pizza in Naples without actually going there.

Ingredients	Regular	Metric
Pizza dough	12" round	30 cm
Olive oil	2 tbsp.	30 ml
Tomatoes, peeled and chopped	4	4
Oregano	1/2 tsp.	2 ml
Mozzarella cheese, grated	4 oz.	125 ml
Anchovies, chopped	6	6

1. Preheat oven to 450°F./230°C.
2. Roll out pizza dough and place on a pizza pan, making a lip around the edge with your fingers.
3. Brush the surface with olive oil, then spread the tomatoes evenly over the surface and sprinkle with oregano.
4. Put grated cheese over tomatoes, and scatter anchovy bits on top.
5. Cook in the oven for 20 minutes, or until crust has browned and cheese has melted. Cut into wedges and serve.

Serves 2-4

Tomato/Pomodoro

All dishes labled *napoletana* contain tomatoes, as the people of Naples lay undisputed claim to the invention of tomato sauce at the end of the 17th century. The tomato itself, a food natural to North America, is believed to have been brought to Italy by European explorers in the 16th century. At that time it was small and yellow so the Italians called it *pomo d'oro*, or "apples of gold", and although Italian horticulturists have bred the tomato into its current large red state, the name *pomodoro* or *pomidoro* still endures.

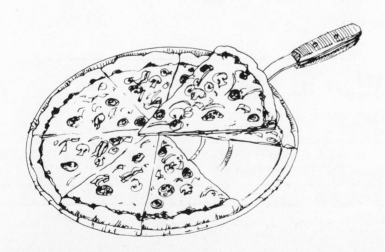

Pizza alla Pasquale

Pizza with Clams, Green Peppers and Mushrooms

This is my favorite pizza. We cook this one at home all the time.

Ingredients	Regular	Metric
Pizza dough	12" round	30 cm round
Tomato sauce	1 cup	250 ml
Baby clams, drained and chopped	10 oz. can.	300 ml
Green pepper, sliced	1/2	1/2
Mushrooms, sliced	6	6
Mozzarella cheese, grated	4 oz.	125 ml
Parmesan cheese, grated	1 oz.	25 ml

1. Preheat oven to 450°F./230°C.
2. Roll out pizza dough and place on a pizza pan, making a lip around the edge with your fingers.
3. Spread tomato sauce over the surface and place baby clams evenly on top.
4. Distribute the green pepper slices and mushrooms, and scatter the mozzarella over them.
5. Sprinkle parmesan over everything, then cook in the oven for 20 minutes or until the crust is golden brown and the cheese has melted. Cut into wedges and serve.

Serves 2-4

Riso al Limone

Rice with Egg and Lemon

This rice dish is lighter and more tender than the standard risotto, because it is cooked in water immediately, whereas risotto is fried in butter first, making it chewier.

Ingredients	Regular	Metric
Rice	1 cup	250 ml
Water	2 1/2 cups	625 ml
Salt	1/2 tsp.	2 ml
Eggs	3	3
Juice of 1 lemon		
Parmesan cheese, grated	6 oz.	200 ml

1. Bring water to a boil, and stir in rice and salt. Lower the heat, cover the pot, and leave to cook for 20 minutes, or until rice is tender.
2. Beat eggs, lemon juice and cheese together. Stir into the rice for several minutes and then serve.

Serves 4

Polenta con Funghi

Polenta with Sausage and Mushrooms

Polenta is one of the most popular dishes in Northern Italy. It is usually served with a sauce of meat, fish or vegetables.

Ingredients	Regular	Metric
Chicken stock	3 cups	750 ml
Salt	1 tsp.	5 ml
Cornmeal	1 cup	250 ml
Oil	2 oz.	50 ml
Fresh sausage	1 lb.	500 g
Mushrooms, sliced	1 lb.	500 g
Tomatoes, peeled and chopped	3	3
Salt	1/2 tsp.	2 ml
Pepper	Pinch	Pinch
Parmesan cheese, grated	5 oz.	125 ml

1. Bring half the stock to a boil with the salt.
2. Mix the cornmeal with the rest of the stock until it is absorbed, then slowly add this mixture to the boiling stock, whisking constantly.
3. Simmer on the lowest heat for 20-30 minutes, stirring often. When it is done, it will form a crust on top and peel away from the pan.
4. Prepare sauce by removing the sausage from the casing, and cooking with the mushrooms in oil for 5 minutes.
5. Add tomato, salt and pepper, and simmer for 20 minutes.
6. Put polenta on heated platter, pour sauce over and top with grated cheese. Serve immediately.

Serves 4-6

Breakfast a'la Minute

In the south of Italy, green peppers are sometimes eaten for breakfast like this. Put some cut-up sausage, bacon or pancetta in a pan with a little oil, and fry quickly for several minutes. Add peppers and potatoes (fresh or left-over) sliced very thin, and sprinkle with a little black pepper. Cook and stir quickly for several more minutes, then serve.

Saffron/Zafferano

Saffron is the most expensive spice in the world, so it is fortunate that so little is needed to make classic dishes like Risotto Milanese.

The spice comes from the stigmas of the saffron crocus. There are three stigmas in each crocus, and they must be removed meticulously by hand and treated gently. Since it takes the stigmas of between 70,000 and 80,000 crocuses, which must also be picked by hand, to make 1 pound of saffron, its price is not so surprising. Unfortunately, some of the ground varieties available can be diluted with an inferior type of saffron which is grown in Mexico, so it is always wise to buy this spice with the stigmas still whole.

Usually 4-6 stigmas are enough for most recipes. Grind them yourself, and then soak in about 2 oz. of hot water before adding to other ingredients. Always cook at a moderate heat so that it doesn't become bitter.

Turmeric is sometimes substituted for saffron by people who think they are saving money and not losing anything else. What they are losing, though, is the unique flavor and distinctive aroma of the real thing, and this is a shame since such a little saffron goes such a long, delicious way.

Risotto alla Milanese

Rice with Saffron

This is the most famous of all risottos, and is traditionally served with Ossobucco.

Ingredients	Regular	Metric
Butter	2 tbsp.	30 ml
Onion, chopped	1	1
Beef marrow (optional)	1/2 cup	125 ml
Rice	1 cup	250 ml
White wine	6 oz.	200 ml
Chicken stock	2 cups	500 ml
Saffron	Pinch	Pinch
Butter	1 tbsp.	15 ml
Parmesan cheese, grated	2 tbsp.	30 ml

1. Heat the butter in a large pot, and cook the onion slowly along with the beef marrow if available, for 5 minutes.
2. Add the rice, and stir for about 3 minutes, until all the fat is absorbed and the rice is still light and translucent.
3. Add the wine and stir until it is absorbed, then bring the stock to a boil and stir in 1 cup slowly.
4. Continue to add the hot stock in small quantities, letting the rice soak in the last addition before adding more.
5. When the rice reaches a creamy consistency, stir in the saffron.
6. After about 25 minutes the rice should be done. Continue to stir until the last minute so that it doesn't stick to the pan, then add the butter and cheese and let stand for several minutes before serving with a passing dish of grated cheese.

Serves 4

Risotto con Funghi

Risotto with Mushrooms

Risotto cooked with the delicate flavour of mushrooms makes a dish which can be served alone, or as an accompaniment to almost any meat or fish.

Ingredients	Regular	Metric
Butter	4 tbsp.	60 ml
Onion, chopped	1	1
Garlic clove, minced	1	1
Mushrooms, sliced	8	8
Oil	2 tbsp.	30 ml
Rice	1 cup	250 ml
Chicken stock	2 cups	500 ml
Salt	1/2 tsp.	2 ml
Pepper	Pinch	Pinch
Parsley, chopped	1 tsp.	15 ml
Parmesan cheese, grated	2 oz.	50 ml

1. Heat 2 tablespoons of butter in a frying pan and cook the onion, garlic and mushrooms for 5 minutes.
2. Heat 2 tablespoons of butter and the oil in a pot and add the rice. Cook and stir until the rice is golden—about 3 minutes.
3. Heat the stock to boiling and add one cup to the rice. Keep stirring until all the liquid has been absorbed, then add onion, mushrooms and seasonings.
4. Keep stirring and adding stock until rice is fully cooked—about 15-20 minutes.
5. Remove from heat and stir in the parsley, cheese, and remaining butter. Let stand for a few minutes, then serve.

Serve 4-6

Rice/Riso

In Northern Italy, rice is as important to a meal as pasta is in the South, and so it is no surprise that a classic dish is *risotto*. Rice was known in regions of Italy in the Middle Ages, but it wasn't until the 16th century that it began to be cultivated successfully, and now the many varied ways of cooking it make it an unforgettable part of the cuisine.

The secret of risotto is the way the hot liquid is added to the sautéed rice – slowly, so that the grains of rice swell, but still retain a chewy, *al dente* quality. It is important to keep stirring the mixture all during the cooking process, but particularly at the end. Otherwise, the rice would stick to the bottom of the pan.

Rice is usually served as a separate course, except in the case of *Risotto alla Milanese* which is traditionally served with Ossobucco, but it also makes a delicious accompaniment to many other dishes. Risotto is very versatile, and can be made with any number of different ingredients, which are integrated into the cooking of the rice. Chicken, shrimp, sausage, chicken livers, ham, and all kinds of seafood are excellent. The best kind to use is an Italian rice like Arborio, but any good long-grain rice is fine.

Risotto Verde

Green Italian Rice

This risotto is delicious with the addition of carrot, celery, spinach and mushrooms—and is hearty enough for a main dish. The parsley adds a fresh taste, as well as contributing to the beautiful green color.

Ingredients	Regular	Metric
Butter	6 tbsp.	90 ml
Onion, chopped	1	1
Carrot, grated	1	1
Celery stalk, thinly sliced	1/2	1/2
Spinach, raw and chopped	3 tbsp.	45 ml
Mushrooms, sliced	4	4
Olive oil	2 tbsp.	30 ml
Rice	1 cup	250 ml
Nutmeg	Pinch	Pinch
Salt	1/2 tsp.	2 ml
Pepper	Pinch	Pinch
Hot chicken stock	3 cups	750 ml
Parsley, chopped	1 tbsp.	15 ml
Parmesan cheese, grated	2 oz.	50 ml

1. Heat 2 tablespoons of butter in a frying pan, and cook the onion for 5 minutes until golden.
2. Add the other vegetables and cook for 5 minutes more.
3. Heat the oil and 2 tablespoons of butter in a pot and stir in the rice. When it is golden, add the vegetables and seasonings.
4. Add 1 cup of boiling stock and keep stirring until the liquid has been absorbed. Add more stock as needed and keep stirring until the rice is cooked—about 15-20 minutes.
5. When risotto is done, stir in parsley, remaining butter and the grated cheese. Cover and let stand for a few minutes and then serve.

Serves 4-6

Gnocchi con Formaggio

Potato Dumplings with Cheese

Most countries of the world have a potato dumpling of some kind, and this is the Italian version which is called "gnocchi".

Ingredients	Regular	Metric
Potatoes	4 lbs.	2 kg
Salt	1 tsp.	5 ml
Eggs	4	4
Nutmeg	Pinch	Pinch
Flour	2 cups	500 ml
Butter	4 tbsp.	60 ml
Fontina or brick cheese	4 oz.	125 g
Pepper	Pinch	Pinch
Tomato sauce	1 cup	250 ml
Parmesan cheese, grated	4 oz.	125 ml

1. Boil potatoes in their skins for 20-30 minutes, then peel and mash until smooth.
2. Beat in half the salt, the eggs and nutmeg, then gradually add the flour until you have a smooth, elastic dough which comes away from the sides of the bowl.
3. Divide into small pieces and roll on a lightly floured surface until you have a rope as thick as a finger, then cut into 1"/2 cm pieces.
4. Drop gnocchi into salted, boiling water. When they rise to the surface, they're done—about 5 minutes. Remove and drain.
5. Heat oven to 400°F./200°C. Place gnocchi in baking dish and put butter on top. Slice enough cheese to cover, then season with the rest of the salt and some pepper.
6. Cook in the oven for 15 minutes or until cheese browns on top, then place on individual serving dishes and cover with heated tomato sauce. Sprinkle with grated cheese and serve immediately.

Serves 4-6

Gnocchi

You can cook gnocchi the way they are cut, or do this:

   1) Put your thumb on the small piece of dough, and pull it toward you – causing the gnocchi to curl up.

   2) Roll the gnocchi along the tines of a fork to create ridges.

   3) Put both thumbs on the dough and press down, making two indentations and a ridge down the middle.

These methods give the gnocchi interesting shapes which look attractive, and do a good job of holding the sauce.

Gnocchi Variations

Gnocchi Gratinati. Heat the oven to 400°F. while you cook and drain the gnocchi. Place them in a baking dish, and put dabs of butter on top, about 4 tablespoons in all. Layer 4 oz. of sliced fontina or brick cheese on top, sprinkle with salt and pepper, and cook in the oven for 15 minutes, or until the cheese is golden brown on top. Serve with tomato sauce, and a sprinkling of grated parmesan.

Gnocchi con Ragu. Cook the gnocchi, and serve with meat sauce and grated cheese for a complete meal.

Gnocchi Verde. Make the gnocchi as usual, but add one pound of spinach (cooked, drained and chopped finely) to the dough. Add a little more flour if necessary. Serve with tomato sauce and grated cheese.

FISH
Pesci

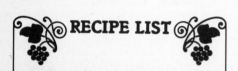
Fish can be used in a variety of ways – in soups, stews, as appetizers and in the *piatto di mezzo* or main course.

Seafood is especially popular in Italy because of the great stretches of excellent fishing waters which surround the country. What the Italians can't catch, they import – including lobster and salmon from Canada and the United States.

When we talk about seafood we mean both fish and shellfish, which includes mollusks and crustaceans. Mollusks have no claws or tails, just two shells. Popular mollusks are mussels, clams, and oysters. Crustaceans, which do have claws and tails, include the members of the crab and lobster families.

Fish is an excellent source of protein, B vitamins and minerals, and it doesn't have to be cooked to be tender. The only reason we cook it is to warm it up and separate it into flakes. No fish should ever be cooked too long because the heat will cause the flesh to become dry and tasteless due to lost juices, and shellfish when overcooked can get really tough and rubbery.

With modern shipping methods, fresh fish can now be found in most places. A good idea, if you live inland, is to find a knowledgeable local fishmonger who can help you in your choices. Remember that a fresh product and a light cooking touch will give you a delicious fish dish every time.

Cozze al Pomodoro

Mussels with Tomatoes

Mussels, simmered in white wine and a bed of tomatoes, with just a hint of chili pepper and oregano.

Ingredients	Regular	Metric
Mussels	24	24
Olive oil	4 tbsp.	60 ml
Green onions, chopped	4	4
Garlic cloves, chopped	2	2
Tomatoes, peeled and chopped	2	2
White wine	4 oz.	125 ml
Oregano	1/2 tsp.	2 ml
Salt	1/2 tsp.	2 ml
Pepper	Pinch	Pinch
Chili peppers	Pinch	Pinch
Parsley, chopped	2 tbsp.	30 ml

1. Scrape the mussels and remove beards, then wash and scrub very well until no trace of sand remains.
2. Heat the oil in a large pot, and cook the onion and garlic for 5 minutes.
3. Stir in the tomatoes, wine and seasonings, and simmer for 5 minutes.
4. Add the mussels and cook, covered, until they open. Serve sprinkled with chopped parsley.

Serves 4

► *If you buy mussels and find you can't use them right away, just store them in the refrigerator, still in their shells, covered with water and milk. This will keep them fresh for three or four days, and make them very plump as well.*

Mussels/Muscioli

Mussels, those black-shelled mollusks with the orange-pink flesh, are gaining rapidly in popularity. They can be grown domestically, or "farmed", which greatly increases their volume, and so reduces the cost. They can be used in stews, soups and salads, but are best steamed in white wine and garlic just until the shells open, and then served in this sweet-smelling sauce.

Fish Stew

This very famous stew is called *cacciucco* along the Mediterranean, but in the Adriatic regions it becomes a *brodetto*. Since this is also the name of the famous bread soup from Venice, things can sometimes get a bit confusing.

It is often eaten as a main course, and can be made even more hearty with the addition of octopus and squid. However it is made, though, it is always served with bread fried in oil, or with croutons.

Cacciucco

Fish Stew

The "cacciucco" is a dish popular in the coastal regions of Italy where fresh fish is readily available. Each region uses the ingredients common to its waters.

Ingredients	Regular	Metric
Olive oil	2 tbsp.	30 ml
Onion, sliced	1	1
Garlic cloves, minced	2	2
Celery stalk, chopped	1	1
Mussels, cleaned	12	12
Cod fillets	2	2
Baby shrimp	10 oz.	300 g
Tomatoes, chopped	4	4
Fish stock	1 quart	1 L
Salt	1/2 tsp.	2 ml
Pepper	Pinch	Pinch
Croutons	1 cup	250 ml

1. Heat the oil in a large pot and cook the onion, garlic and celery for 5 minutes.
2. Cut the cod into small bite-size pieces, and add to the pot along with the well-scrubbed mussels and baby shrimp. Cook until the mussel shells open, then add the tomatoes and stock.
3. Simmer for 20 minutes, then season with salt and pepper and serve topped with croutons.

Serves 4

Filetti di Sogliola Mandorle

Fillets of Sole with Almonds

For the most tender and delicate taste, try to use the real Dover sole in this dish. The fillets are quite small though, so plan to use one whole fish per person.

Ingredients	Regular	Metric
Oil	2 tbsp.	30 ml
Butter	2 tbsp.	30 ml
Sole fillets	4	4
Flour	2 tbsp.	30 ml
Salt	1/2 tsp.	2 ml
Pepper	Pinch	Pinch
Mushrooms, sliced	12	12
Juice of 2 lemons		
White wine	2 oz.	50 ml
Almonds, sliced	4 oz.	125 ml
Parsley, chopped	1 tbsp.	15 ml

1. Heat two frying pans—one with oil, and one with butter.
2. Dredge sole in flour, salt and pepper, then cook in oil for 2 minutes each side.
3. Cook mushrooms in butter for 4 minutes, then add to the fish.
4. Add remaining ingredients and simmer for 5 minutes. Remove fish and place on heated platter, then pour sauce on top. Serve with wedges of lemon.

Serves 4

Sole/Sogliola

Some of the sole sold in North America is actually flounder. Real sole comes from Europe and is called Dover Sole or English Sole. Since it must be flown in on ice, it is often more expensive than local sole or flounder, but has a better taste and texture.

▶ *Many restaurants include fresh fish dishes on their menus, and some restaurants even specialize in fish and seafood. If you have enjoyed a particular fish recipe, don't hesitate to ask the owner where his fish is usually obtained. This is often the best way of discovering new suppliers and good fishmongers.*

1. A Dover Sole has four fillets — two on each side. First, slice across the tail end, and lift up the skin with your knife.

2. Hold the tail of the fish with one hand, and grab the skin with the other. Now pull the skin away from the fish.

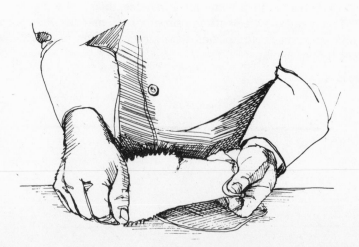

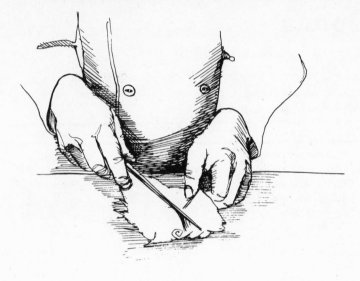

3. Notice the backbone running down the middle of the fish, with one fillet on each side. Slice along the backbone with your knife.

4. Scraping away from the backbone with your knife, lift away the two fillets. Now turn the fish over and repeat the process for the other two fillets.

Fish Stock/Brodo di Pesce

Fish stock is the base for fish soups and chowders, or for sauces to be served with fish, like Lobster Thermidor or Fillets Bonne Femme.

Use as soon after making as you can as it will only keep in the refrigerator for a couple of days, although it will last several weeks in the freezer.

Ask at your fishmonger's for carcasses which are left after filleting, because they are usually just thrown away. Especially good are the heads and bones of white fish like sole, flounder or halibut – sometimes the stronger flavors of mackerel and similar fish are too overpowering – and if you can get the shells from shrimp, crab or lobster, they will add a really special flavor.

    4 lbs. fish scraps, washed
    1 carrot, sliced
    1 onion, sliced
    2 celery stalks with leaves, chopped
    6 peppercorns, crushed
    3 lemons, cut in half, juice and peel
    2 bay leaves

Place all the ingredients in a large soup pot, not aluminum, and cover with cold water, about 4 quarts. Bring to a boil, then skim off the froth and lower the heat. Cook, partially covered, for 30-45 minutes. Don't overcook, or the stock will become sour. Strain through a sieve lined with cheesecloth to remove any fine bones, then boil liquid down to the right consistency and adjust the seasonings. Cool uncovered, and put in the refrigerator covered, or in 2 cup containers in the freezer.

▶ *When keeping any stock in the refrigerator, boil it up for 10 minutes every 2 days to keep it from going sour, and always boil before using it, or adding to it for soup.*

Filetti di Sogliola Buona Donna

Fillets of Sole Bonne Femme

This is a beautiful way to use fish stock. Sole fillets are cooked with white wine, stock and mushrooms, "bonne femme", then served with a mushroom and cream sauce.

Ingredients	Regular	Metric
Skinned sole fillets	1 lb.	500 g
Button mushrooms, caps and stems	1 cup	250 ml
Green onion, minced	1	1
Parsley, chopped	2 tbsp.	30 ml
Dry white wine	4 oz.	125 ml
Fish stock	1 cup	250 ml
Butter	2 tbsp.	30 ml
Flour	1 tbsp.	15 ml
Salt	1/8 tsp.	1 ml
Pepper	Pinch	Pinch
Heavy cream	4 oz.	125 ml

1. Place the fillets in a buttered casserole dish, and cover with the mushroom stems, green onion, half the chopped parsley, the wine and stock.
2. Place in a preheated 375°F./190°C oven for 10-15 minutes until the fish is flaky, then remove to a heated platter.
3. Heat the butter in a saucepan, and add the mushroom caps, whole or halved depending on the size. Cook and shake for 2 minutes.
4. Add the flour, and cook for 1 minute, then strain the cooking juices into the pan very slowly, stirring constantly.
5. Season with salt and pepper, bring to a boil, and cook for 1 minute.
6. Just before serving, stir in the cream and cook until it is heated, then pour the sauce over the fillets and sprinkle with the rest of the chopped parsley. Garnish with parsley sprigs, and serve with new boiled potatoes.

Serves 4

Filetto di Sogliola Dore

Fillets of Sole Dore

Fillets coated in batter, cooked until golden, and served with a velvety smooth butter-lemon sauce.

Ingredients	Regular	Metric
Flour	4 oz.	125 ml
Baking powder	1 tbsp.	15 ml
Salt	1/2 tsp.	2 ml
Pepper	Pinch	Pinch
Milk	3 oz.	75 ml
Eggs	3	3
Sole fillets	2 lbs.	1 kg
Oil	2 tbsp.	30 ml
Butter	1 cup	250 ml
Brandy	1 oz.	25 ml
White wine	2 oz.	50 ml
Juice of 1 lemon		

1. In a bowl, mix flour, baking powder, salt and pepper, breadcrumbs, milk and eggs, then coat sole fillets with the mixture.
2. Heat oil in a frying pan and cook fish for 2 minutes each side until golden brown, then remove to a heated platter.
3. Melt butter in the frying pan. Add brandy, wine and lemon juice. Cook briskly for 2 minutes, the pour over fish and serve immediately.

Serves 4-6

➤ *If you use frozen fish, thaw slowly in the refrigerator until it becomes pliable, then cook it the same way as fresh. This way, the fish will retain its precious moisture, and the texture and flavor will be preserved.*

"You should always view life as if your wine glass is half full, and not half empty."

Fresh Fish

In Italy, fish and seafood are an important part of many meals, and the long coastlines of the Mediterranean and Adriatic seas provide Italians with an astonishing variety of fresh catches daily.

In the inland regions of North America, however, fresh fish has often been hard to find, but this is changing. With the increased interest in good nutrition and tasty low-fat foods, people are beginning to realize the value and versatility of fish, and modern transportation and packing methods are making freshly-caught fish more accesible.

When you are buying fresh fish, you should use three things — your eyes, your nose, your fingers. Look carefully at the fish. It should have a definite gleam in its eye, which should also be bright and firm. The gills should be red, and the scales close to the skin. Next, take a good, deep whiff. The fish should smell fresh — as fresh as the water it came from — and never, never, "fishy". Finally, squeeze the flesh between your fingers and thumb. It should be firm and springy without any of the sliminess which would leave your fingers sticky.

As soon as you select your perfect fish, bring it home at once. Rinse it under cold running water, put it in a plastic bag, and store on ice or in icewater until ready to use.

Filetti di Sogliole Imbotitto

Stuffed Sole in Wine

Use fairly large fillets in this recipe, as the fish has to be rolled around the tomato and cucumber. The grapes add a nice touch to the fresh taste of this dish.

Ingredients	Regular	Metric
Sole fillets	4	4
Cucumber, diced	1/2	1/2
Tomato, peeled and chopped	1	1
Butter	4 tbsp.	60 ml
Green onions, chopped	3	3
White seedless grapes	4 oz.	125 g
White wine	4 oz.	125 ml
Juice of 1 lemon		
Heavy cream	2 oz.	50 ml
Salt	1/2 tsp.	2 ml
Pepper	Pinch	Pinch

1. Place cucumber and tomato on fillets and roll up tightly. Secure with toothpicks.
2. Heat butter in a large frying pan and cook fillets, turning gently until all sides are cooked well.
3. Add green onions, grapes, wine and lemon juice, and cover the pan. Simmer for 10 minutes, then remove fish to a heated serving platter.
4. Add cream to the pan and boil gently for a few minutes until sauce thickens a little. Season to taste with salt and pepper, pour over fish and serve immediately.

Serves 4

Trancie di Salmone con Vegetali

Poached Salmon Steak Jardiniere

Salmon steaks poached until tender, and served with a vegetable sauce which delights the eye as well as the taste.

Ingredients	Regular	Metric
Salmon steaks	4-8 oz. each	4-250 g
Fish or chicken stock	1 cup	250 ml
Juice of 3 lemons		
Onion, sliced thinly	1	1
Carrots, peeled and shredded	2	2
Green pepper, sliced thinly	1	1
White wine	4 oz.	125 ml
Paprika	1 tsp.	5 ml
Salt	1/2 tsp.	2 ml
Pepper	Pinch	Pinch
Butter	2 tbsp.	30 ml
Flour	1 tbsp.	15 ml
Parsley, chopped	1 tbsp.	15 ml

1. Put salmon steaks in a large pan with all the ingredients except the butter, flour and parsley.
2. Cook gently for 10 minutes or until centers come out of the steaks easily. Remove to a heated platter and keep warm.
3. Bring sauce to a boil. Mix butter and flour together and whisk into liquid, then cook and stir for 3 minutes.
4. Pour sauce over fish, sprinkle with chopped parsley, and serve.

Serves 4

► *When poaching whole fish, it is always a good idea to wrap it in a sheet of cheesecloth to help keep the fish in one piece, and make it easier to lift out of the pan.*

▶ *To give hollandaise a wonderful taste, add some sherry to the egg yolks before beating.*

Salmone Bulito

Poached Salmon

Whole salmon, poached in a savory mixture of stock, vegetables and herbs. White wine and lemon juice add the final special touch.

Ingredients	Regular	Metric
Salmon, whole	4-5 lb.	2 kg
Fish or chicken stock	1 quart	1 L
Celery stalk	1	1
Carrot	1	1
Onion	1	1
Leek	1	1
Lemons, juice and peel	2	2
Bay leaves	2	2
Garlic clove	1	1
Thyme	Pinch	Pinch
Parsley sprigs	2	2
White wine	4 oz.	125 ml

1. Preheat oven to 375°F./190°C.
2. Wash the salmon and place on a rack in a large roasting pan, or in a fish poacher.
3. Cover with the stock. Chop the celery and carrot coarsely, and add to the pan. Wash the leek carefully under running water and cut off tough greens. Quarter and add to pan with peeled and quartered onion.
4. Add the rest of the ingredients and cook in the oven for 30-40 minutes until the meat loses its deep pink color around the backbone.
5. Let the fish cool in the liquid, then remove carefully and place on serving platter. Garnish with cooked vegetables, and serve with hollandaise sauce.

Serves 4-6

Hollandaise Sauce/Olandese

Hollandaise sauce is not difficult to make if you remember three things.
1. Beat your yolks well until they are very thick.
2. Heat them very slowly because if they get too hot, they won't absorb the butter.
3. Add the butter slowly.
   5 egg yolks
   Juice of 1 lemon
   Pinch of cayenne
   Pinch of salt
   6 oz. melted butter
Put the yolks, lemon juice, and seasoning in a heavy saucepan, and place over very low heat.
Beat vigorously with a wire whisk until the yolks have thickened and you can begin to see the bottom of the pan between strokes. While you are doing this, take the pan off the heat occasionally so the eggs don't get too hot.
Touch the side of the pan with your hand. If the pan is too hot for your hand, it's too hot for the sauce.
As soon as the eggs are the right consistency, start whisking in the butter very slowly until the mixture is like cream, and all the butter has been added. When the sauce coats the whisk, it's done.
You can keep hollandaise sauce for a short time over a pan of hot water, but it's better to use it as soon as possible.
Makes about 1 cup.

Spigola alla Marinara

Sea Bass with Marinara Sauce

Marinara, "sailor style", is a sauce used in southern Italy with tomatoes, garlic and oil. This recipe features bass, but many different kinds of fish can be substituted.

Ingredients	Regular	Metric
Bass fillets	4	4
Flour	4 tbsp.	60 ml
Olive oil	4 tbsp.	60 ml
White wine	2 oz.	50 ml
Marinara sauce	2 cups	500 ml
Peppercorns, crushed	2 tbsp.	30 ml
Parsley, chopped	2 tbsp.	30 ml

1. Dredge the fillets in flour and shake off the excess.
2. Heat the oil in a large frying pan and cook the fish for 4 minutes, or until golden brown on each side.
3. Add wine, sauce and pepper. Simmer for 10 minutes, then place on a warm platter with sauce on top. Sprinkle with parsley and serve.

Serves 4-6

➤ *Cook fish for ten minutes per inch at its thickest part.*

Pesco al Cartoccio

Fish Cooked in Foil

The original recipe for this dish called for the fish to be cooked in a paper bag or "cartoccio". But foil is much better because it seals in all the juices and steams the fish to flaky tenderness.

Ingredients	Regular	Metric
Whole fish, salmon, trout, bass	4 lbs.	2 kg
Juice of 1 lemon		
Butter	1 tbsp.	15 ml
Bacon drippings	1 tbsp.	15 ml
Parsley sprigs	3	3
Salt	1/2 tsp.	2 ml
Pepper	Pinch	Pinch

1. Place fish on a large piece of foil and add all the other ingredients.
2. Fold the foil around the fish and seal the edges tightly.
3. Place under coals and cook for 20 minutes, or on a barbecue grill for 20-30 minutes. In a 375°F./190°C oven, cook for 20 minutes, or 10 minutes for each inch/2 cm at the thickest part. Test for doneness before serving.

Serves 4-6

Bianchetti Fritti

Fried Small Fish

This is a very easy way to cook little fish of any kind. Use sardines, smelts, anchovies, whitebait, or a combination. This can be served as an appetizer as well.

Ingredients	Regular	Metric
Small fish	2 lbs.	1 kg
Flour	1 cup	250 ml
Salt	1/2 tsp.	2 ml
Pepper	Pinch	Pinch
Garlic powder	1/2 tsp.	2 ml
Oregano	1/2 tsp.	2 ml
Oil for frying		
Parsley, chopped	1 tbsp.	15 ml
Lemons, quartered	2	2

► *When cooking meat or fish, never add salt until the last minute. Salt toughens the fibers, especially in seafood.*

► *If you buy anchovies which have been packed in oil, remove and drain well. Then dip them in a little egg, coat in flour, and cook for several minutes in some hot olive oil until they are golden brown. Serve with lots of crusty bread and a couple of glasses of wine for a tasty and satisfying light meal.*

1. Wash the fish and dry thoroughly.
2. Dredge in flour seasoned with salt and pepper, garlic powder, and oregano. Shake off excess.
3. Heat plenty of oil in a deep-frying pan until it is hot enough to cook a small square of bread golden brown almost immediately. Drop fish into the oil and cook until they are brown and crisp—about 2 minutes. Remove and drain well.
4. Continue until all the fish are done, then serve with parsley and lemon wedges.

Serves 4

Baccala al Pomodoro

Salt Cod with Tomatoes

This is a popular and tasty dish which is also inexpensive and savory. Salt cod is stewed until just tender and flaky in tomatoes and wine flavored delicately with herbs.

Ingredients	Regular	Metric
Baccala fillets	2 lbs.	1 kg
Flour	4 oz.	125 ml
Olive oil	3 tbsp.	45 ml
Onion, chopped	1	1
Garlic cloves, chopped	2	2
Tomatoes, peeled and chopped	4	4
Ground black pepper	Pinch	Pinch
Chili peppers	Pinch	Pinch
Thyme	Pinch	Pinch
Basil	Pinch	Pinch
Bay leaves, crumbled	2	2
White wine	4 oz.	125 ml

1. Soak the cod, then cut in 2"/5 cm pieces and dredge in flour.
2. Heat the oil in a large frying pan, then cook the cod until golden on both sides, turning once.
3. Add the onion and garlic. Cook for a few minutes more, then add all the other ingredients and cook, covered, for 20 minutes or until fish flakes easily. Place on heated platter and serve.

Serves 4-6

Baccala

Baccala, dried cod fish, was introduced to the Mediterranean region by the Normans, and has remained a popular Lenten dish in many regions.

It must be soaked in cold water for two days before cooking, and the water should be changed twice a day. Even so, the dish will probably be salty enough without adding any extra, so be sure to taste any dish containing baccala before seasoning.

Gamberi con Limone

Shrimp with Lemon Sauce

A very attractive dish of shrimps on a bed of lettuce with a creamy and colorful sauce in the middle. This also makes an excellent appetizer.

Ingredients	Regular	Metric
Shrimp	24	24
Juice of 1 lemon		
Tomato paste	1 tbsp.	30 ml
Brandy	2 oz.	50 ml
Salt	1/2 tsp.	2 ml
Pepper	Pinch	Pinch
Heavy cream	4 oz.	125 ml
Tabasco sauce	4 drops	4 drops
Worcestershire sauce	4 drops	4 drops
Apple, peeled and chopped	1	1
Parsley, chopped	1 tsp.	5 ml
Iceberg lettuce, shredded	2 cups	500 ml
Lemon wedges	4-6	4-6

1. Cook shrimp and cool, then shell and devein leaving the tails on.
2. Meanwhile, mix the lemon juice, tomato paste, brandy and seasonings together in a bowl.
3. Whip the cream until it is stiff, then fold into the mixture with the next 4 ingredients.
4. Put shredded lettuce in the bottoms of large cocktail glasses, and stand the shrimps up around the sides.
5. Spoon sauce into the middle, and serve with lemon wedges.

Serves 4-6

Cooking Shrimp

It is always better to cook shrimp in their shells so the flavor of the shells enters the meat. Here's the best way to do it.
1) Bring one quart of water to a boil with a little lemon juice, and cook the shrimp for three minutes.
2) Just before removing, stir in a splash of white wine vinegar, then plunge the shrimp into cold water to stop them cooking.
3) Peel, and devein by running the tip of a knife or a toothpick down the center of the back.
The most important thing to remember is, never add salt to the cooking water as it will toughen the fish.

Gamberi alla Cavaliere

Broiled Shrimp Cavaliere

Jumbo shrimp, marinated in a sauce of wine, mustard and lemon, are cooked on the grill and served on a bed of rice.

Ingredients	Regular	Metric
Oil	4 tbsp.	60 ml
Melted butter	4 tbsp.	60 ml
White wine	4 oz.	125 ml
Parsley, chopped	2 tbsp.	30 ml
Dry mustard	1 tsp.	5 ml
Oregano	1 tsp.	5 ml
Juice of 2 lemons		
Jumbo shrimp, peeled and deveined	1 1/2 lbs.	750 g

1. Combine ingredients and marinate shrimps for 30 minutes.
2. Arrange shrimp on a large piece of aluminum foil, and place on an outdoor grill or under the broiler. Cook for 3-5 minutes on each side and serve with rice.

Serves 4

Shrimp/Gamberi

There are hundreds of different kinds of shrimps, but the most important difference between them is usually how big or small they are. The best size for many recipes is 16-20, which means that there are 16 to 20 fish per pound. Varieties smaller than this are sweet and tender, and very good in salads.

Shrimp are available canned or frozen, but for cooking, fresh is always better for taste and texture as long as they aren't over-cooked, and are drained immediately so that they don't toughen up. Usually, one pound of shrimp in the shell, without heads, gives about 3/4 pound of meat.

If you buy fresh shrimp in the shell, look for ones that fit tightly into their shells, have a firm texture, and smell fresh and not fishy. Sometimes the fish have been frozen and then thawed out. These will look shrunken, and be limp and unshiny. Stay away from them as the taste will not be the same.

Very large or jumbo shrimp are some-times called prawns, which is a bit confusing as the real prawn is actually a member of the lobster family and includes the delicious Italian variety called scampi, but whatever they are called, jumbo shrimp are very pop-ular and excellent for stuffing, or for deep-fat frying.

First, take the shell off the shrimp, leaving the tail. Devein by running a sharp knife down the back, and scraping out the vein with a toothpick or the knife's end. To but-terfly, continue the cut without going all the way through, and flatten. Coat in bread-crumbs or batter, and deep-fry at 375°F. for 5-8 minutes or until golden. Another inter-esting shape can be achieved by making three deep gashes across the back, flattening, then cooking the same way.

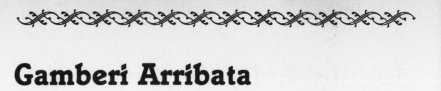

Gamberi Arribata

Hot Shrimps

Sautéed shrimps in a hot tomato sauce with sage and lemon.

Ingredients	Regular	Metric
Shrimps, large	24	24
Flour	4 oz.	125 ml
Olive oil	4 oz.	125 ml
Onion, chopped	1	1
Garlic cloves, chopped	2	2
Sage	1/2 tsp.	2 ml
Tomato sauce	1 cup	250 ml
Beef stock	2 oz.	50 ml
Butter	2 tbsp.	30 ml
Chili pepper	1/2 tsp.	2 ml
Juice of 1 lemon		
Tabasco sauce	4 drops	4 drops

1. Peel and devein the shrimp, then toss in the flour and set aside.
2. Heat half the oil in a large frying pan and cook the onion, garlic and sage for 5 minutes. Add the next 6 ingredients and simmer for 10 minutes.
3. In another frying pan, heat the rest of the oil until very hot. Add the shrimp and cook, shaking the pan continuously, for about 2 minutes.
4. Stir the shrimp into the sauce and serve over a bed of rice.

Serves 4-6

"Music and food go together. Working with food is like being a composer — you must have imagination for both."

Code d'Aragosta al Brandi

Lobster Tails with Brandy Sauce

An elegant dish of red lobster tails swimming in a sauce of wine, brandy and spiced stock.

Ingredients	Regular	Metric
Lobster tails	8-6 oz. each	8-200 g
Oil	4 tbsp.	60 ml
Butter	4 tbsp.	60 ml
Paprika	1 tbsp.	15 ml
Breadcrumbs	4 tbsp.	60 ml
Brandy	4 oz.	125 ml
White wine	4 oz.	125 ml
Chicken stock	4 oz.	125 ml
Onion, choppped	1	1
Sage	1/2 tsp.	2 ml
Peppercorns, crushed	1/2 tsp.	2 ml
Juice of 4 lemons		
Dry mustard	1/2 tsp.	2 ml
Salt	1/2 tsp.	2 ml

1. Wash lobster tails, split down the backs and butterfly.
2. Heat oil and butter in a large frying pan and cook lobster for 5 minutes, meat side down.
3. Add remaining ingredients and simmer for 15 minutes, until the shells turn pinkish red.
4. Remove tails and place in heated serving dish. Boil sauce gently for 5 minutes until it has reduced slightly, then pour over lobster and serve.

Serves 4

Lobster/Aragosta

Most of the lobster tails you buy to cook at home are the tails from the spiny or rock lobster – *langasta* or *langouste* – which differ from the more famous North American *homard* lobster by their lack of claws. They come from warmer waters so their meat is less desired, but it is also less expensive and more readily available.

They are usually frozen, and it is very important to thaw them completely and slowly in the refrigerator so they won't lose any moisture, then bring them to room temperature before cooking.

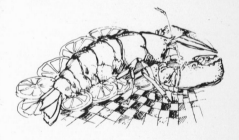

Aragosta Fra Diavola

Lobster and Hot Sauce

This is a little more expensive than other dishes, but so good that it's worth it. It should be hot and red like the devil or "diavola".

Ingredients	Regular	Metric
Lobster tails	4	4
Olive oil	2 tbsp.	30 ml
Onion, finely chopped	1	1
Garlic clove, minced	1	1
Curry powder	1/4 tsp.	1 ml
Basil	1/4 tsp.	1 ml
Cayenne	Pinch	Pinch
Oregano	1/4 tsp.	1 ml
Chili peppers	Pinch	Pinch
Tabasco	4 drops	4 drops
Tomatoes, peeled and chopped	3	3
Red wine	4 oz.	125 ml
Salt	1/2 tsp.	2 ml
Pepper	Pinch	Pinch
Parsley, chopped	1 tbsp.	15 ml

1. Remove lobster meat from tails.
2. Heat oil in a large frying pan, and cook the meat until pink.
3. Add onion and garlic, and cook for a few minutes more, then add the next 8 ingredients and lower heat. Cover and simmer for 10-15 minutes.
4. Season to taste with salt and pepper, stir in parsley, and serve with rice.

Serves 4

Ostriche in Umido

Creamed Oyster Stew

Plump oysters, cooked in their own juice, cream and celery, and colored with paprika and parsley.

► *When buying oysters, select young ones – those with the least number of shell rings – of uniform size, and be sure to rap on the shells. If the oyster is healthy, the shell will immediately snap shut.*

Ingredients	Regular	Metric
Butter	4 tbsp.	60 ml
Onion, minced	1	1
Garlic clove, minced	1	1
Celery stalk, chopped	1	1
Oysters with liquid	24	24
Milk	1 cup	250 ml
Salt	1/2 tsp.	2 ml
White pepper	Pinch	Pinch
Heavy cream	1 cup	250 ml
Egg yolks, beaten	2	2
Paprika	1/2 tsp.	2 ml
Parsley, chopped	1 tbsp.	15 ml

1. Heat butter in a pot and cook the onion, garlic and celery for 5 minutes.
2. Take oysters from shells and place them and their liquid in a pot with the milk. Simmer over low heat until liquid becomes hot and the oysters float on the top. Season with salt and pepper.
3. Mix the cream and egg yolks together, and pour slowly into the stew. Cook on very low heat, stirring constantly until sauce thickens.
4. Remove from the heat and stir in the paprika and parsley. Let sit for 1 minute, then serve.

Serves 4-6

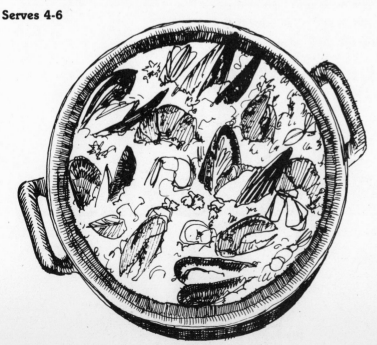

Oyster/Ostriche

To open or shuck an oyster, first wash the shell thoroughly, then wrap a small towel around one hand to prevent injury. Take the oyster in this hand, flat side up, and hold an oyster knife in the other.

Insert the point of the knife between the shells at the narrow end, and twist the knife in this hinge until the shell opens. Separate the oyster from the upper shell by cutting the muscle at the top and running the knife around the rim, then discard the top, and scrape the oyster meat away from the bottom. If eaten raw, serve in the bottom shell with just the natural juice, or a little lemon added.

Squid/Calamari

Squid meat is very popular in the Mediterranean regions because of its distinctive taste and chewy texture. If you cook it too long, though, this texture will become like rubber.

Young squid are the best for cooking. Buy them fresh and whole for the finest taste. The eyes should be bright, and the fish should smell like sea-water with firm flesh which is not at all sticky.

Cutting up Squid

1. Cut the tentacles away from the main body with a sharp knife.

Calamari in Padella

Fried Squid

This method of pan frying turns the squid into a very light, crisp dish which can also be used as an appetizer.

Ingredients	Regular	Metric
Squid, cleaned and peeled	8	8
Flour	1/2 cup	125 ml
Sage	1/2 tsp.	2 ml
Pepper	Pinch	Pinch
Oil	4 oz.	125 ml
White wine	2 oz.	50 ml
Juice of 2 lemons		
Butter	1 tbsp.	15 ml
Salt	1/2 tsp.	2 ml
Parsley, chopped	1 tbsp.	15 ml

1. Cut squid into bite-size pieces, and dredge in flour seasoned with sage and pepper.
2. Heat the oil in a frying pan and cook the squid for about 5 minutes, stirring occasionally.
3. Add the wine, lemon juice and butter, then simmer for 5 minutes and season to taste with salt.
4. Stir in parsley and serve immediately.

Serves 4

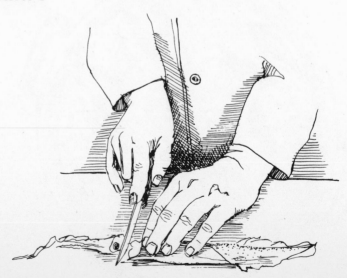

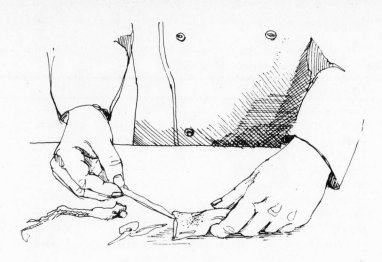

2. Reach inside the body and pull away the cartilage.

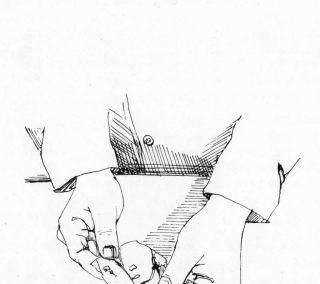

3. Pull off the skin and now slice up for cooking.

Vongole alla Fiorentina

Clams Florentine Style

Clams baked in a creamy Bechamel sauce, flavored with brandy and leeks, and topped with bubbling cheese.

Ingredients	Regular	Metric
Cherrystone clams	24	24
Oil	2 tbsp.	30 ml
Butter	2 tbsp.	30 ml
Onion, chopped	1	1
Leek, white only, chopped	1	1
Garlic cloves, chopped	2	2
Spinach, chopped	1 lb.	500 g
White wine	4 oz.	125 ml
Brandy	4 oz.	125 ml
Bechamel sauce	1 cup	250 ml
Bacon slices, chopped	4	4
Mozzarella, shredded	4 oz.	125 ml
Parmesan, grated	4 oz.	125 ml
Parsley, chopped	1 tbsp.	15 ml
Chili powder	1/2 tsp.	2 ml
Oregano	1/2 tsp.	2 ml
Sage	1/2 tsp.	2 ml
Lemon wedges	6-8	6-8

1. Preheat oven to 500°F./260°C.
2. Wash clams well and place in a baking dish with a little water in the bottom. Cook in oven until the shells open, then remove and lower the heat to 350°F./180°C.
3. Remove the clam meat and chop, reserving the shells.
4. Heat the oil and butter in a large frying pan and cook the onion, leek and garlic for 5 minutes. Add spinach and cook 3 minutes more.
5. Stir in chopped clam meat, liquids and Bechamel sauce. When bubbling, add cheeses, parsley and seasonings.
6. Fill 24 shell halves with this mixture and put back into baking dish, without water this time.
7. Put in the oven and cook for 20 minutes or until the tops are golden brown. Serve immediately with lemon wedges.

Serves 6

Bechamel Sauce/Balsamilla

This is a wonderfully versatile sauce which can be used with vegetables, fish, and in many baked pasta, *pasta al forno*, dishes.
  4 tbsp. butter
  4 tbsp. flour
  2 cups of milk
  Salt
  Small pinch cayenne
  Small pinch nutmeg
You can make this sauce in any quantity as long as you remember to add 1/2 cup of milk for every tablespoon of flour. First, put the butter into a heavy saucepan, and melt slowly so that it doesn't brown, then stir in the flour. Let it bubble until it begins to froth. Take off the heat and let cool for a minute, then whisk the milk in slowly until all the milk has been added and the sauce is smooth with no lumps. For a better consistency heat the milk first. Put it back on the heat, and continue to whisk until the mixture thickens. Cook and stir for another few minutes, then season to taste.
Makes 2 cups

Conchiglie Rosolate con Pernod

Scallops with Pernod

A small dash of Pernod adds just the right amount of zip to the delicate flavor of scallops in this easily prepared dish.

Ingredients	Regular	Metric
Oil	2 tbsp.	30 ml
Scallops	2 lbs.	1 kg
Flour	4 tbsp.	60 ml
Butter	2 tbsp.	30 ml
Green onions, chopped	2	2
Paprika	1/2 tsp.	2 ml
Juice of 1 lemon		
White wine	2 oz.	50 ml
Pernod	1 tbsp.	15 ml
Cream	4 oz.	125 ml
Parsley, chopped	1 tbsp.	15 ml

1. Heat oil in a large frying pan. Dredge scallops in flour, then cook in oil until golden brown on both sides.
2. Add butter and green onion and cook for 2 minutes, then stir in paprika, lemon juice and wine. Simmer for 3-5 minutes.
3. Remove scallops to a heated platter and add cream to the pan. Boil gently for a couple of minutes until the sauce has thickened slightly. Pour sauce over scallops and sprinkle with chopped parsley.

Serves 4-6

Scallop/Conchiglie

The only part of the scallop we usually eat is not the fish at all, but the large muscle which attaches the fish to the conch shell. This muscle is called the *foot* and varies in size from the sweet and juicy bay scallop, which is about 1/2 inch in diameter, to the larger and chewier sea scallop.

When buying scallops, sniff for a nice fresh smell, feel for a firm and shiny flesh which bounces back, and never overcook or they will become tough. If you find you have to hold up the dinner for some reason, take the scallops out of the pan, then shake them up quickly on high heat just before serving.

CHICKEN

Pollo

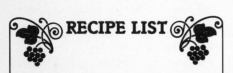
Chicken has always been the symbol of a full larder, prosperity, and safety from hunger. Henry IV of France became famous for his wish in the 16th century that there should be a chicken in every pot in every home in France.

Before modern marketing techniques, chicken used to be quite expensive and a Sunday luxury, but nowadays in North America, it is readily available at prices which would have made King Henry smile, although it is still considered a delicacy in Italy.

Like the egg, the chicken is incredibly versatile, and you could cook a chicken dish every week for a year and never repeat yourself. Not only is it a rich source of B vitamins, it is also a wonderful low-fat, high protein food containing the lowest number of calories per pound of any meat, with the added advantage of being very easy to digest.

Every country in the world appreciates the delicious merits of chicken, and every country has its own recipes, including Italy. Generally speaking, chicken is simmered in white wine in the North, while in the South it is often cooked with tomatoes and herbs. It can be an everyday kind of food, and then suddenly, with a little dressing up, an "extravaganza" or special occasion dish.

Many cooks believe, wrongly, that the longer you cook chicken, the tenderer it will be. Unfortunately, the opposite is true. The longer chicken is cooked, the tougher it gets, until finally it is stringy, dry and tasteless. Cook only until done, and no longer.

In this section, the recipes are mostly for chicken, but there are also some for duckling and turkey. Turkey has become quite sought after in Italy – a welcome gift from North America which is supposed to have been brought back by the Jesuits.

Petti di Pollo al Marsala

Chicken Breasts with Marsala Wine

Chicken breasts are boned and breaded, then simmered to tender perfection in Marsala wine.

Ingredients	Regular	Metric
Chicken breasts	3	3
Salt	1/2 tsp.	2 ml
Pepper	Pinch	Pinch
Eggs	2	2
Breadcrumbs	1 cup	250 ml
Parmesan cheese, grated	2 oz.	50 ml
Butter	2 oz.	50 ml
Olive oil	2 tbsp.	30 ml
Marsala wine	1 cup	250 ml

1. Skin, bone, and cut chicken breasts in half. Pound lightly to flatten.
2. Beat salt and pepper into eggs. Combine breadcrumbs and grated cheese.
3. Dip chicken in the egg mixture, then coat well with breadcrumbs.
4. Heat butter and oil in a large frying pan, and cook the chicken for 2-3 minutes on each side until light golden.
5. Add Marsala, cover and reduce heat. Cook gently for 15-20 minutes, turning occasionally.
6. Remove chicken to heated platter, adjust seasonings in sauce, pour over chicken and serve.

Serves 4-6

▶ *You should always try to buy fresh chicken instead of frozen, as the freezing and defrosting processes break down the fibers of the flesh and tend to make the chicken mushy. If you have no choice but to buy it frozen, then make sure it is as hard as a rock with no frost on the outside. When you're ready to use it, defrost it very slowly in the refrigerator.*

Boned Chicken Breasts

You can buy chicken breasts already boned for chicken scaloppine and other dishes, but they cost more than chicken on the bone. Try boning them yourself like this.

1) Ask the butcher to split the breast in two, or do it yourself with a sharp knife or poultry shears.
2) Pull the skin off, and remove any extra fat.
3) Slip a small, sharp knife between the flesh and the ribcage, and gently scrape the meat away — helping with your fingers.
4) Remove the small bone on the underside, and press the meat together in case the fillet has become separated from the rest of the breast.

Now you can pound into thin scaloppine or leave as is, whatever the recipe calls for.

Petti di Pollo alla Panna

Chicken in Cream

Everyone will think you are a master chef when you cook this elegant dish which is really very easy.

Ingredients	Regular	Metric
Chicken breasts, split	4	4
Flour	4 oz.	125 ml
Salt	1/2 tsp.	2 ml
Pepper	Pinch	Pinch
Oil	2 tbsp.	30 ml
Curry powder	1/4 tsp.	1 ml
Chicken stock	6 oz.	200 ml
Sherry	2 oz.	50 ml
Heavy cream	4 oz.	125 ml
Parsley, chopped	1 tbsp.	15 ml

1. Skin and bone chicken breasts, then pound lightly to flatten. Dredge in flour seasoned with salt and pepper.
2. Heat oil in a large frying pan and cook chicken for 4 minutes on each side.
3. Add curry, chicken stock, sherry and cream, and simmer for 10 minutes.
4. Remove chicken to heated platter and bring sauce to a boil. Let it reduce until thick, adjust seasonings, and pour over the chicken.
5. Sprinkle with parsley and serve.

Serves 4-6

Chili Peppers/Peperoni

Chili peppers originated in the New World, although there are now over 200 different varieties grown. They got their name from the Indian word *chilli*, and from Christopher Columbus who thought at first that they were peppercorns. He must have realized his mistake fairly quickly, though, when he tasted them, as all kinds of chili peppers have one thing in common — they're hot!

Once the explorers brought them back to Europe, their popularity spread to nearly every cuisine in the world, including the Italian. Products for cooking which contain chili peppers are Tabasco sauce, paprika, cayenne pepper, and the flaked red peppers called for so often in Italian recipes.

This dried chili pepper keeps its punch much longer if it is tightly capped and kept in the refrigerator.

Pollo Arribita

Broiled Chicken with Spices

Chicken, marinated in a special sauce and cooked on the grill, makes a tasty summer dish.

Ingredients	Regular	Metric
White wine	4 oz.	125 ml
Oil	4 oz.	125 ml
White vinegar	2 oz.	50 ml
Green onions, chopped	2	2

Oregano	1 tsp.	5 ml
Rosemary	1 tsp.	5 ml
Sage	1 tsp.	5 ml
Peppercorns, crushed	1 tsp.	5 ml
Garlic powder	1/2 tsp.	2 ml
Chili powder	1/2 tsp.	2 ml
Salt	1/2 tsp.	2 ml
Pepper	1/4 tsp.	1ml
Chicken parts	4 lbs.	2 kg
Orange slices		

1. Combine ingredients and marinate chicken pieces for 2 hours.
2. Place a sheet of foil on the grill and shape it like a boat to catch the juices.
3. Arrange chicken on top, and cook for about 20 minutes each side, basting often with juices and some of the marinade.
4. When chicken is done, serve with orange slices.

Serves 4-6

Pollo al Forno con Limone

Roasted Lemon Chicken

Chicken rubbed with oil and tarragon, and roasted with lemons. The oil in the lemon rinds is released constantly as the chicken cooks, giving this dish a fresh and zesty flavor.

Ingredients	Regular	Metric
Chicken	4 lb.	2 kg
Olive oil	4 tbsp.	60 ml
Tarragon	1 tsp.	5 ml
Salt	1 tsp.	5 ml
Lemons	2	2

1. Preheat oven to 350°F./180°C.
2. Wash chicken inside and out, and dry thoroughly. Rub skin with oil, sprinkle with tarragon and salt, and place in roasting pan.
3. Cut lemons in half and squeeze juice over the top of the bird. Cut halves into smaller pieces and place in pan.
4. Roast in oven for $1^1/_2$-2 hours, basting occasionally.
5. Remove chicken and let sit for 10 minutes before carving to let the juices settle.

Serves 4-6

Tarragon/Targone

Tarragon leaves lose a lot of their flavor when dried, so if possible, buy fresh leaves and keep them in a large amount of red or white wine vinegar. Then you can use both the leaves and the beautifully flavored vinegar whenever you need them.

Parmesan/Parmigiano

Parmesan cheese is probably the best-known Italian cheese. After a lengthy period of draining and drying, it emerges as an excellent hard cheese which will keep for years. It is superb for cooking because it doesn't become sticky when melted, and its slightly salty taste and fine grain when grated make it a perfect cheese for sprinkling on pasta.

Buy a large chunk and grate it as you need it, then wrap tightly between uses and keep refrigerated.

Petti di Pollo Soppresa

Chicken with Eggplant and Cheese

This is the original "chicken parmigiana" recipe from Parma. The eggplant and mozzarella make this dish both authentic and delicious.

Ingredients	Regular	Metric
Chicken breasts, halved	3	3
Flour	4 oz.	125 ml
Salt	1/2 tsp.	2 ml
Pepper	Pinch	Pinch
Eggs, beaten	3	3
Table cream	3 oz.	75 ml
Breadcrumbs	1 cup	250 ml
Olive oil	4 tbsp.	60 ml
Eggplant, peeled	1	1
White wine	4 oz.	125 ml
Tomato sauce	4 oz.	125 ml
Parmesan cheese, grated	4 tbsp.	60 ml
Mozzarella cheese slices	8	8 slices
Butter	2 tbsp.	30 ml

1. Preheat oven to 350°F./180°C.
2. Skin and debone the chicken, pound lightly to flatten, then dredge in flour seasoned with salt and pepper.
3. Mix the eggs and cream together and dip the chicken breasts in this liquid, then pat in the breadcrumbs until evenly coated.
4. Heat oil in a large frying pan and cook the breasts for 3 minutes on each side, then remove to a large baking dish.
5. Cut peeled eggplant into slices $1/4$"/1 cm thick, dip in cream and egg, then in breadcrumbs. Put in the frying pan and cook for 1 minute each side in the same oil. Remove and place on the chicken breasts.
6. Add the wine, tomato sauce and grated parmesan to the chicken and sprinkle with salt and pepper, then lay the mozzarella cheese slices on top to cover.
7. Dot with butter and cook in the oven for 10-15 minutes, or until the cheese is completely melted and lightly browned on top.

Serves 4-6

Pollo con Funghi

Chicken with Mushroom Sauce

Chicken breasts in a creamy mushroom sauce, lightly seasoned.

Ingredients	Regular	Metric
Chicken breasts, split	4 lbs.	2 kg
Flour	4 oz.	125 ml
Salt	1/2 tsp.	2 ml
Pepper	Pinch	Pinch
Oil	2 oz.	50 ml
Butter	2 oz.	50 ml
Mushrooms, sliced	1 lb.	500 g
Chicken stock	1 cup	250 ml
Juice of 1 lemon		
White wine	1 cup	250 ml
Nutmeg	1/4 tsp.	1 ml
Heavy cream	6 oz.	200 ml
Parsley, chopped	1 tbsp.	15 ml

1. Dredge the chicken pieces in flour seasoned with salt and pepper.
2. Heat the oil and butter in a large frying pan and cook the chicken until well-browned all over, about 7-10 minutes.
3. Lower the heat and continue to cook the chicken for another 20-30 minutes, turning occasionally until chicken is evenly cooked and tender. Remove to a heated platter and keep warm.
4. To the same pan, add the mushrooms and a little more butter if necessary, and cook for 5 minutes.
5. Add the stock, lemon juice and wine, and boil vigorously for 2 minutes, scraping any bits from the bottom of the pan. Lower the heat and stir in the nutmeg and cream, then continue to cook until sauce has thickened slightly. Pour over chicken and serve sprinkled with parsley.

Serves 4-6

▶ *Cook small mushroom caps very quickly in butter, shaking the pan, until they are golden but still crisp. Add a splash of dry white wine, and bring to a boil. Cook 1 minute and serve.*

"Never serve too much food in one course. If you're still not full, go on to another course of something different. Remember that the best spice in life is variety."

Cutting up Chicken

Chicken parts are handy if you just want one or two for a small meal, but often it is better and more economical to buy a whole chicken and cut it up into parts yourself. Get a 2-3 pound broiler-fryer, and do this.

1) Turn the bird on its breast, and with a pair of poultry shears or a very sharp knife, cut along each side of the backbone as closely as possible, then remove it and turn the chicken over.

2) Cut through the ribs on one side of the breastbone until the bird is in two parts.

3) Pull each leg away from the chicken's body, and slice through the leg joint with a sharp knife, then pull and keep cutting until the leg is off. Now, cut through the joint in the middle of the leg for thigh and drumstick parts.

4) Slit the skin at the top of the wing, and move the wing back and forth until you can find a place to cut through the joint, then cut the tips off if you wish.

5) Now you have eight parts you can use in recipes, plus the neck, backbone, and wingtips left for making stock.

Pollo Stufato

Chicken with Wine and Mushrooms

In Italy, stufato is a type of stew which can also be made with beef or veal. In this recipe, chicken is cooked until tender in red wine and mushrooms.

Ingredients	Regular	Metric
Chicken parts	3 lbs.	1 1/2 kg
Flour	4 oz.	125 ml
Oil	2 tbsp.	30 ml
Butter	4 tbsp.	60 ml
Mushrooms, sliced	1 lb.	500 g
Bacon, chopped	2 oz.	50 ml
Red wine	1 cup	250 ml
Oregano	Pinch	Pinch
Tomato paste	1 tbsp.	15 ml
Beef stock	1 cup	250 ml
Salt	1/2 tsp.	2 ml
Pepper	Pinch	Pinch
Parsley, chopped	2 tbsp.	30 ml

1. Dredge the chicken parts in flour, reserving 2 tablespoons.
2. Heat the oil and half the butter in a large pot and cook the chicken until golden brown all over—about 10 minutes.
3. Add the mushrooms and bacon, and cook until the fat on the bacon is done thoroughly but is not crisp.
4. Add the next 6 ingredients and cook over medium heat, partially covered, for 20-30 minutes, or until the meat comes away from the bone.
5. Remove chicken and place on a heated platter. Bring the sauce to a boil, mix the remaining butter and flour together, and whisk into the liquid until the sauce thickens.
6. Adjust seasonings, pour over chicken, and serve with the parsley sprinkled on top.

Serves 4-6

Pollo alla Cacciatore

Chicken with Wine and Vegetables

Hunter-style or "cacciatore" means meat cooked with a lot of vegetables. Although chicken has become the most popular "cacciatore", pork, veal, and even liver can be prepared this way.

Ingredients	Regular	Metric
Chicken parts	4 lbs.	2 kg
Flour	4 oz.	125 ml
Olive oil	4 tbsp.	60 ml
Onion, chopped	1	1
Garlic cloves, minced	2	2
Green pepper, sliced	1	1
Mushrooms, sliced	10	10
Tomatoes, peeled and chopped	3	3
Tomato paste	2 tbsp.	30 ml
White wine	4 oz.	125 ml
Chicken stock	6 oz.	200 ml
Bay leaf, crumbled	1	1
Basil	Pinch	Pinch
Salt	1/2 tsp.	2 ml
Pepper	Pinch	Pinch

1. Dredge the chicken lightly in flour.
2. Heat the oil in a large pot and cook the chicken for 7-10 minutes, until golden brown all over.
3. Add the onion, garlic, green pepper and mushrooms, and cook for 3 minutes more.
4. Add the other ingredients, cover and simmer gently for 30-45 minutes, or until chicken is tender. Adjust seasonings and serve immediately.

Serves 4-6

▶ *Keep leftover tomato paste from drying out by covering it with a little oil, and storing in the refrigerator.*

Spezzatino di Pollo

Chicken in Tomato and White Wine Sauce

Tender young chicken goes into a covered skillet, and cooks slowly in tomatoes and wine until ready to fall off the bone.

Ingredients	Regular	Metric
Butter	4 tbsp.	60 ml
Oil	4 tbsp.	60 ml
Chicken, cut up	4 lbs.	2 kg
White wine	4 oz.	125 ml
Tomatoes, peeled and mashed	1 lb.	500 g
Garlic clove, crushed	1	1
Parsley, chopped	1 tbsp.	15 ml
Oregano	Pinch	Pinch
Salt	1/2 tsp.	2 ml

1. Heat the butter and oil in a large frying pan and cook the chicken for 5-7 minutes until golden brown on all sides. Remove from pan and keep warm.
2. Pour the wine into the pan and bring to a boil, scraping bits from the bottom of the pan. Add remaining ingredients, cook for 2 minutes, then lower the heat and put the chicken back in the pan.
3. Cover the pan and let chicken cook gently for 45 minutes, then adjust seasonings and serve.

Serves 4-6

Deglazing

This is the method used to rescue all the tasty, cooked-on bits left on the bottom of the pan after frying so you can make a delicious and simple sauce. This way, none of the tastes are wasted.

First, remove the fish, fowl, or meat, then add a little wine or stock to the frying pan. As it simmers, stir up the browned residues, and then either pour over the dish as is, or add cream and other ingredients to form a richer sauce.

Pollo alla Marengo

Chicken Marengo

A famous but simple dish of chicken pieces browned in olive oil and garlic, and simmered until tender in tomatoes, mushrooms and white wine.

Ingredients	Regular	Metric
Chicken pieces	4 lbs.	2 kg
Oil	3 tbsp.	45 ml
Butter	3 tbsp.	45 ml
Onion, chopped coarsely	1	1

Garlic clove, minced	1	1
Mushrooms	10	10
Tomatoes, peeled and chopped	4	4
Thyme	1/4 tsp.	1 ml
Oregano	1/4 tsp.	1 ml
Bay leaf, crumbled	2	2
Chicken stock	6 oz.	200 ml
White wine	4 oz.	125 ml
Juice of 1 lemon		
Wine vinegar	2 oz.	50 ml.
Salt	1/2 tsp.	2 ml
Pepper	Pinch	Pinch

1. Heat the oil and butter in a large pot and cook the chicken until golden brown all over, about 5 minutes each side.
2. Add the onion, garlic and mushrooms, and cook for another 3-5 minutes.
3. Add all the other ingredients, except the salt and pepper, and cover.
4. Simmer gently for 30-45 minutes, or until the chicken is tender, then remove meat to a heated serving platter.
5. Add salt and pepper to sauce and bring to a boil. When it has reduced by half, pour it over the chicken and serve immediately.

Serves 4-6

➤ *When you are buying fresh poultry, press on the breastbone to test for freshness. If it is soft, the bird is young and the meat will be moist and tender.*

Chicken Marengo

After Napoleon's victory at Marengo, Spain in 1800, he ordered his chef to prepare something very special to eat. Supplies were scarce, but the quick-thinking chef culled all he could from neighboring farms, then added ingredients found growing in the earth close at hand. The resulting dish, Chicken Marengo, was such a success that Napoleon requested it on many other occasions — thus ensuring its place in culinary history.

Pollo alla Giardinera

Fried Chicken with Herbs

Chicken seasoned with different herbs and spices, and served up on a cool bed of lettuce for a nice presentation.

Ingredients	Regular	Metric
Chicken pieces	6-8	6-8
Basil	1 tsp.	5 ml
Tarragon	1 tsp.	5 ml
Oregano	Pinch	Pinch
Rosemary	Pinch	Pinch
Bay leaves, crumbled	2	2
Garlic powder	1 tsp.	5 ml
Pepper	Pinch	Pinch
Oil	4 oz.	125 ml
Salt	1/2 tsp.	2 ml
Parsley, chopped	2 tbsp.	30 ml
Lettuce, shredded	1/2 head	1/2 head
Lemon wedges	8	8

1. Season the chicken with the first 7 ingredients.
2. Heat the oil in a large pot and cook the chicken for 7-10 minutes, or until golden brown all over.
3. Cover the pot, lower the heat, and cook for another 20-30 minutes.
4. Season with salt and parsley and cook for 5 minutes more, then serve on a bed of lettuce with lemon wedges on the side.

Serves 4-6

➤ *If you must use dried herbs in a recipe, rub them first in the palm of your hand with a sprig of fresh parsley. This will greatly enhance the flavor and bring out the beautiful aroma.*

➤ *When you are getting chicken or chicken parts which have been packaged, watch out for liquid lying on the bottom, as this probably means that the meat was frozen and then thawed.*

Petti di Pollo in Carrozza

Stuffed Chicken Breasts

Tender white meat wrapped around cheese and ham, and cooked in a creamy wine sauce.

Ingredients	Regular	Metric
Chicken breasts	3	3
Prosciutto or ham slices	6	6
Fontina cheese slices	6	6
Milk	1 cup	250 ml
Flour	1 cup	250 ml
Salt	1/2 tsp.	2 ml
Pepper	Pinch	Pinch
Butter	2 oz.	50 ml
White wine	1 cup	250 ml
Heavy cream	2 oz.	50 ml
Parsley, chopped	1 tbsp.	15 ml

1. Skin, bone, and split chicken breasts in half, then pound lightly to flatten.
2. Place a slice of ham and a slice of cheese on each breast. Roll up and secure with a toothpick.
3. Dip chicken into milk, then into flour seasoned with salt and pepper.
4. Heat butter in a large frying pan and cook chicken until golden on all sides, then add the wine, reduce heat, and cover the pan. Simmer gently for 20 minutes until the chicken is tender, turning several times while cooking, then remove to a heated platter.
5. Bring the sauce to a boil and scrape any bits from the bottom of the pan. Take off the heat, add the cream and adjust the seasonings, and spoon over the chicken. Sprinkle with parsley and serve immediately.

Serves 4-6

Fontina

Fontina is a famous Italian cheese made in Piedmont. It is mild-tasting, buttery, and creamy – similar to the Gruyere of Switzerland. It is very good to eat alone, but is usually used melted in cooking, especially in a fondue dish called Piedmontese fonduta.

➤ *Chicken is perishable, and can go bad very quickly, but these rules will help things go right.*
1. Store chicken in the refrigerator, lightly covered with paper so the air can get to it, and use as soon as possible, at least within a day or two.
2. Never leave chicken out at room temperature for any length of time – even to thaw.
3. After cutting up chicken, wash the cutting surface down with hot soapy water, or you may affect other foods and end up with a sore stomach.

Oregano

Oregano is a form of marjoram, although much more pungent. It first became known in North America for its peppy taste on pizzas, but it is also good with lamb, soups and fish. It goes very well with basil, and is delicious with all kinds of Mediterranean vegetables, like tomatoes, eggplant, zucchini and olives.

It is much more potent dried than fresh, and if it is kept in a cool, dark place, it will keep its flavor for a long period of time. Use sparingly, and taste before adding more.

Pollo alla Greglia

Chicken with Oregano

Chicken pieces are broiled until tender with a sauce of lemon and oregano.

Ingredients	Regular	Metric
Chicken pieces	4 lbs.	2 kg
Salt	1/2 tsp.	2 ml
Pepper	Pinch	Pinch
Juice of 1 lemon		
Olive oil	4 oz.	125 ml
Garlic clove, minced	1	1
Parsley, chopped	1 tbsp.	15 ml
Oregano	2 tsp.	10 ml

1. Preheat broiler and place rack 6"/15 cm beneath it.
2. Wash chicken and coat thoroughly with all the other ingredients.
3. Place on broiler pan and cook under broiler for 15-20 minutes on each side basting occasionally with the juices.
4. When chicken is brown and tender, serve with the pan juices poured over.

Serves 4-6

Arrosto di Tacchino

Roast Turkey

This way of cooking turkey gives you a beautiful moist bird, and a delicious gravy. Some people like to truss the turkey before cooking, but I never do because I think it's a waste of time. My turkeys always seem to roast very well on their own without being all tied up.

Ingredients	Regular	Metric
1 fresh turkey	12 lbs.	5½ kg
Apple, peeled and cored	1	1
Celery stalks	2	2
Salt	2 tbsp.	30 ml
Pepper	2 tbsp.	30 ml

Garlic powder	1 tbsp.	15 ml
Gin	4 oz.	125 ml
Bacon slices	6	6
White wine	4 oz.	125 ml
Chicken stock	1 cup	250 ml

1. Preheat the oven to 500°F./250°C.
2. Wash and dry the turkey, inside and out, then cut the apple and celery into large chunks and place inside the bird.
3. Put in a large roasting pan, and cover with the next 4 ingredients.
4. Lay the bacon slices over the breast, and roast in the oven for 30 minutes.
5. Remove, and lower the temperature to 400°F./200°C.
6. Take the bacon slices off, and put in the bottom of the pan along with the wine and stock, then put the bird back in the oven for about 90 minutes.
7. Test for doneness, then put turkey on a heated platter for 20 minutes before carving to let the juices settle, and make the gravy.

Serves 6

► *To prepare poultry for roasting, you must always wash the bird inside and out with salt water, then rinse with very cold water and dry thoroughly.*

Gravy

This method works well with both roasted chicken and turkey.

   1 1/2 cups pan juices
   1 1/2 cups chicken stock
   3 tablespoons flour
   6 tablespoons water
   Salt
   Pepper
   2 tablespoons chopped parsley

Separate the fat from the meat juices, pour the juices back into the roasting pan with the chicken stock, and bring to a boil. Mix the flour and water together into a smooth paste, and add to the pan very slowly, whisking constantly. When the mixture is thick and smooth, season to taste with salt and pepper, then stir in the parsley and serve.
Makes 3 cups

Anatroccollo Arosto con Cilegie

Roast Duckling with Cherry Sauce

Ducklings cooked for a special occasion with a colorful and mouth-watering sweet and sour sauce of cherries, cherry brandy and lemon juice.

Ingredients	Regular	Metric
Ducklings	2-3 lbs. each	2-1$^1/_2$ kg each
Garlic cloves	2	2
Salt	1/2 tsp.	2 ml
Pepper	Pinch	Pinch
Lemon	1/2	1/2
Onion, quartered	1	1
Celery stalk, halved	1	1
Chicken stock	1 cup	250 ml
Brown sugar	4 oz.	125 ml
Vinegar	2 tbsp.	30 ml
Cherry brandy	4 oz.	125 ml
Cherries, pitted	12 oz. can	375 ml can
Cornstarch	2 tbsp.	30 ml

1. Preheat oven to 375°F./190°C.
2. Wash and dry ducklings and prick skins all over. Rub with garlic, sprinkle with salt and pepper, and place in a roasting pan.
3. Squeeze the lemon, and put the juice in a bowl and the rinds in the pan with the ducklings, along with the onion and celery, then cook in the oven for 90 minutes, or until the internal temperature reaches 180°F./90°C in the thickest part of the thigh. Prick skins during cooking to release fat.
4. When ducklings are cooked, remove to a heated platter and cut in half.
5. Discard vegetables and pour off fat, then place pan on top of the stove and add chicken stock. Bring to a boil and scrape the bits from the bottom of the pan, then continue to cook until stock is reduced by half.
6. In another pan, heat the sugar until just melted. Add the vinegar, cherry brandy, and cherries with juice. Boil rapidly until slightly reduced, then add lemon juice.

Duck with Orange Sauce

Cook just the same way as Duck with Cherry Sauce, except add to the melted sugar:
   1 cup orange juice
   2 oz. lemon juice
   2 oz. Grand Marnier
Then proceed as before. If you can get Seville oranges, it makes the dish even better. Use the juice, and then slice one orange very thinly into the sauce as it cooks.

7. Dissolve cornstarch in a little cold water and add to the sauce. Strain the chicken stock into the sauce and cook gently until slightly thickened. Pour over ducklings and serve.

Serves 4

Anatroccollo con Olivo

Duckling with Olives

An unusual recipe from the Liguria region of Italy which has the reputation of growing the finest olives, and making the best olive oil. In this dish, you should use fresh, green olives if you can find them—otherwise pickled ones will be fine.

Ingredients	Regular	Metric
Duckling	5 lbs.	2 1/2 kg
Salt	1 tsp.	5 ml
Sage	1/2 tsp.	2 ml
Pepper	Pinch	Pinch
Onion, chopped	1	1
Chicken stock	2 cups	500 ml
Green olives, pitted	6 oz.	200 ml
Duck liver	1	1

1. Preheat oven to 550°F./290°C.
2. Wash and dry ingredients, then rub cavity with salt and sage, and outside with salt and pepper. Prick skin all over.
3. Put duckling in roasting pan and cook in the oven for 15 minutes.
4. Remove, pour off fat, and lower temperature to 450°F./230°C.
5. Put the onion, stock and olives in the pan and cook in the oven, basting often and pricking the skin to let the fat out, for 1 1/2 hours.
6. Half an hour before it is done, add the liver, cut in 6 pieces.
7. When duckling is done, carve on heated platter. Skim as much fat as possible from the juices in the pan. To serve, spoon the remaining ingredients in the pan over the duckling slices.

Serves 4-6

Olive/Oliva

Although there are over 35 different species of olive, basically there are two types used for eating and cooking – green ones and black ones.

Black olives are picked ripe, and used as a relish or appetizer, whereas green olives are picked before they are fully ripe, and have many uses.

In Italy, they are either served fresh, or pickled in brine, and taste excellent stuffed with anchovies or pimento. They are used in antipasto dishes, as a garnish, and, in some regions, as an ingredient in cooking.

BEEF

Manzo

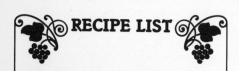
Beef is the most popular meat in North America, and even in Italy, a rib-roast or *rosbiffe* is a fine dish for company or a special family get-together.

Whenever you buy beef, look at the fat. It should be white and crumbly, and there should be a good deal of it. This proves that the animal has spent life eating its head off in a barn, and not galloping up and down in some field developing tough sinews and muscles.

In North America, there are two distinct types of beef – Canadian and American. Canadian beef has been bred over the years for leaness. This has the advantage of lowering cholesterol and calories, but the meat sometimes lacks the natural tenderness of the fatter and more finely marbled meat of its southern cousins. Whatever type or cut of beef you choose, treat it gently, cook it properly, and eat it slowly . . . and you'll enjoy every bite.

Bistecca alla Fiorentina

Steak with Spinach

Make sure you're really hungry when you cook this dish—there's a lot of meat in these steaks, and it's too good to waste.

Ingredients	Regular	Metric
Olive oil	4 tbsp.	60 ml
Parsley, chopped	2 tbsp.	30 ml
Sage	1 tsp.	5 ml
Nutmeg	1 tsp.	5 ml
Oregano	1 tsp.	5 ml
Garlic powder	1 tsp.	5 ml
Salt	1 tsp.	5 ml
Pepper	1/2 tsp.	2 ml
T-bone or striploin steaks	4-12 oz. each.	4-375 g each
Juice of 2 lemons		
Lemon wedges	4	4
Spinach, cooked and drained	1 lb.	500 g

1. Combine first 8 ingredients and marinate steaks for at least 2 hours.
2. Grill over white-hot coals for 6 minutes each side, basting with lemon juice.
3. Serve with lemon wedges and buttered spinach.

Serves 4

Florentine/Fiorentina

When Catherine de Medici travelled from Florence to marry French King Henry II, she brought her chefs and all their secrets with her. They, in turn, introduced spinach to French cooking, and since then, any recipe which contains this vegetable is named *florentine* or *fiorentina* after the beautiful city of Florence.

Marinade/Marinate

Cheaper cuts of meat can be tenderized and made delicious by soaking them in a marinade for a period of time. The marinating liquid can then be used to cook the meat in, or added to the final sauce.

Count on about 1/2 cup of marinade for every pound of meat. Cubed meat needs to be soaked for a couple of hours, but a larger piece would benefit from staying in the liquid overnight. The marinade not only adds flavor of its own, but brings out and spreads the flavor of the meat itself.

A marinade always contains an acid to break down the tough fibers, and some kind of oil to help spread the flavors – because of the acid, you should never put the marinating liquid in an aluminum bowl or pan.

If you're going to soak anything for more than an hour, put the whole thing in the refrigerator, and be sure to turn the meat over every once in a while so that all the sides are tenderized.

Wine marinade

1/2 cup red wine, or red wine vinegar
1/4 cup water
Juice of 1/2 lemon
2 tablespoons chopped onion
1/2 teaspoon tarragon
Freshly ground pepper
1 bay leaf
1/2 cup olive oil

Beer marinade

1 cup flat beer
1/2 cup oil
2 cloves garlic
Juice of 1/2 lemon
1/2 teaspoon salt
1 tablespoon sugar or honey

Braciola di Manzo al Vino

Beef Roll in Wine Sauce

This is an excellent way to cook an inexpensive cut of beef. You can vary the stuffing by adding a spoonful of minced pinenuts.

Ingredients	Regular	Metric
Round steak	1 lb.	500 g
Garlic clove, minced	1	1
Parmesan cheese, grated	2 tbsp.	30 ml
Breadcrumbs	4 tbsp.	60 ml
Hard-cooked egg, chopped	1	1
Parsley, chopped	1 tbsp.	15 ml
Raisins	2 tbsp.	30 ml
Salt	1/2 tsp.	2 ml
Pepper	Pinch	Pinch
Oil	4 oz.	125 ml
Onion, sliced	1	1
Tomato paste	1 tbsp.	15 ml
Tomatoes, peeled and chopped	3	3
Basil	1/2 tsp.	2 ml
Bay leaf, crumbled	1	1
Red wine	4 oz.	125 ml

1. Pound steak until it is $1/4$"/$1/2$ cm thick.
2. Mix the next 6 ingredients together and spread over the beef, then season with salt and pepper. Roll beef up, jelly-roll fashion, and secure the join with toothpicks.
3. Heat the oil in a pot and cook the onion for 5 minutes until golden.
4. Add the beef roll and cook until browned all over, then add remaining ingredients. Cover the pot and simmer gently for $1\frac{1}{2}$-2 hours.
5. Remove the roll, slice crossways and serve with the sauce poured on top.

Serves 4-6

Medaglioni di Manzo

Medallions of Beef in Red Wine Sauce

Tender medallions of beef in a creamy wine sauce makes an elegant dish, perfect for special meals.

Ingredients	Regular	Metric
Beef tenderloin	2 lbs.	1 kg
Flour	4 oz.	125 ml
Salt	1/2 tsp.	2 ml
Pepper	Pinch	Pinch
Oil	4 tbsp.	60 ml
Butter	2 tbsp.	30 ml
Onion, chopped	1	1
Bacon slices, chopped	4	4
Mushrooms, quartered	12	12
Brandy	2 oz.	50 ml
Beef stock	6 oz.	200 ml
Soft butter	1 tbsp.	15 ml
Flour	1 tbsp.	15 ml
Red wine	2 oz.	50 ml
Heavy cream	2 oz.	50 ml

1. Cut the beef into 1"/2 cm slices, then dredge lightly in flour seasoned with salt and pepper.
2. Heat the oil and butter in a large frying pan, and sear the beef for 2 minutes on each side, then lower the heat to medium and add the onion, bacon and mushrooms. Cook for 5 minutes.
3. Add the brandy and flame, then pour in the beef stock and simmer for 3 minutes.
4. Remove meat to heated platter and bring the sauce to a boil. Mix the flour and butter together and whisk into the boiling liquid until it has thickened, then add wine and cream and cook another 2 minutes.
5. Adjust seasonings, pour over meat, and serve immediately.

Serves 4-6

► *Never pierce a piece of beef while it is cooking, or the juices will run out and be lost. When cooking steak, turn only once, and always use tongs.*

"I am never rough with a good cut of steak. I treat it as gently as if I were touching the face of a beautiful woman."

Polpette Casalinga

Spicy Meatballs

I call these hot and spicy meatballs "casalinga", or home-style, because this is the way we used to cook them in my home in Italy. They are delicious served with your favorite pasta and sauce.

Ingredients	Regular	Metric
Ground beef	2 lbs.	1 kg
Garlic cloves, minced	2	2
Basil	1 tsp.	5 ml
Chili peppers	1 tbsp.	15 ml
Nutmeg	1/2 tsp.	2 ml
Pepper	1 tsp.	5 ml
Salt	1/2 tsp.	2 ml
Tomato paste	2 tbsp.	30 ml
Breadcrumbs	4 oz.	125 ml
Parsley, chopped	2 tbsp.	30 ml
Eggs	3	3

> ➤ *To see whether the mixture is the right consistency for meatballs, here is a simple test. Make a shape like a golfball, and put it in the palm of your hand. Then turn your hand over, and if the ball sticks, the consistency is just right.*

1. Mix the first 10 ingredients together in a bowl.
2. Using your hands, add the eggs one by one until the mixture is the right consistency. If mixture is not moist enough after all the eggs have been added, mix in a little red wine.
3. Oil your hands and roll the meat into balls with your palms. Place them in a roasting pan with a little water in the bottom. Cook in a preheated 350°F./180°C oven for 20 minutes, taste to see if they are done, and then serve.

Serves 4-6

Arrosto di Manzo alla Pasquale

Roast Beef Italian Style

Roast beef has always been considered a typically English dish, so the name came into the Italian language as "rosbiffe". This particular way of cooking it, however, is all my own, and produces a roast which is both tender and tasty.

Ingredients	Regular	Metric
Rib roast	6 lbs.	3 kg
Salt	2 tbsp.	30 ml
Pepper	2 tbsp.	30 ml
Garlic powder	1 tbsp.	15 ml
Dry mustard	1 tbsp.	15 ml
Water	8 oz.	250 ml
Red wine vinegar	4 oz.	125 ml
Red wine	4 oz.	125 ml

1. Preheat the oven to 475°F./240°C.
2. Put meat in roasting pan, fat side up, and insert a meat thermometer at the thickest part.
3. Rub seasonings into the meat and cook in the oven for 45 minutes.
4. Turn the heat down to 350°F./180°C and let pan cool for about 10 minutes before adding liquids.
5. Place back in the oven and cook for 1 hour more, or until the meat thermometer registers the degree of doneness you prefer. Baste several times during cooking.
6. Remove the meat to a heated platter and let stand for 10-15 minutes to let the juice settle, then carve and serve with pan juices as gravy.

Serves 8

"The best restaurant you can go to in the world is your own home."

123

> ➤ *Putting hard-boiled eggs in the middle of a meatloaf not only makes the slices look and taste wonderful, but also ensures that the loaf is done all the way through, with no uncooked bits in the center.*

The Wines of Italy

We Italians love our wine, and have it at least once every day with our meals, so it's not surprising that more wine is consumed in Italy than in any other country. We make up for it, though, because Italy is also the largest producer of wines in the world.

Some of these, especially the reds, are among the best you can find anywhere, but really, Italy is best known for its inexpensive, everyday vinos. Whatever type you get, make a note of the shipping company when you taste something you really like, and stick with that name whenever you buy other Italian wines.

A guide to all the wines from Italy, a country with so many regions and kinds of grapes, would take up a whole book, so I will give you here just a few of the most popular ones.

Polpettone Pasquale

Pasquale's Special Meatloaf

With the eggs peeking out of the center of the loaf, this makes a very colorful dish. Serve it on a large platter surrounded by vegetables and topped by a tomato sauce if you wish.

Ingredients	Regular	Metric
Ground veal	1 lb.	500 g
Ground beef	1 lb.	500 g
Parmesan cheese, grated	2 oz.	50 ml
Parsley, chopped	2 tbsp.	30 ml
Salt	1/2 tsp.	2 ml
Pepper	Pinch	Pinch
Nutmeg	Pinch	Pinch
Ham or prosciutto, chopped	6 oz.	200 g
Bay leaves, crumbled	2	2
Eggs	4	4
Hard-cooked eggs, peeled	6	6

1. Preheat oven to 350°F./180°C.
2. Combine the first 10 ingredients in a bowl, adding the eggs one at a time until the mixture is moist but not mushy.
3. Divide this mixture into 2 parts and place on separate sheets of oiled aluminum foil. Flatten the meat until it is 1"/2 cm thick, and the length of your baking dish.
4. Put the hard-cooked eggs end-to-end down the center of each portion of flattened meat.
5. Using the foil, fold up each side of the meat around the eggs. Pinch the edges together, and mold into a sealed loaf. Fold the foil around the loaves and seal tightly.
6. Place in a baking dish with a little water in the bottom, and cook in the oven for 1 hour.
7. Remove and let cool for a few minutes, then take off the foil and cut into slices.

Serves 6-8

Bistecca di Manzo al Funghi

Steak with Mushroom Sauce

This is a beautiful way to serve steaks. The meat is cooked until pink and tender inside, and crisp on the outside—then the steaks are covered with a mushroom sauce with consommé, wine and cream.

Ingredients	Regular	Metric
Oil	2 tbsp.	30 ml
Striploin steaks	4-8 oz. each	4-250 g each
Mushrooms, sliced	12	12
Green onions, chopped	2	2
Consommé	4 oz.	125 ml
Flour	1 tbsp.	15 ml
Butter, melted	2 tbsp.	30 ml
Red wine	4 oz.	125 ml
Heavy cream	4 oz.	125 ml
Parsley, chopped	1 tbsp.	15 ml
Salt	1/2 tsp.	2 ml
Pepper	Pinch	Pinch
Nutmeg	Pinch	Pinch

1. Heat oil in a large frying pan and cook steaks for 5 minutes on each side. Remove and keep warm.
2. Add mushrooms and green onions to the pan and cook for 5 minutes.
3. Add consommé, bring to a boil, and let reduce for 3-5 minutes.
4. Mix flour and butter together, whisk into sauce, then cook for 1 minute still stirring constantly.
5. Whisk in the wine, cream, parsley and seasonings. Cook for 3 minutes, then pour over the steaks and serve.

Serves 4

Vino Rosso/Red Wine

Barolo. This is possibly Italy's finest red wine. It comes from the premier grape-growing region of Piedmont in Northern Italy, and is dark-colored and long-lasting.

Barbera. A full-bodied wine, also from the Piedmont region, which is always much in demand.

Castelli Romani. This average but inexpensive wine comes from the vineyards just outside Rome.

Chianti. This is the best-known of all Italian wines and comes from Tuscany. It has a good, robust quality which goes well with hearty dishes, and is an outstanding value for money, especially if you can find it in its distinctive straw-covered bottle. After you have enjoyed the wine, you can use the bottle as a candle holder.

Valpolicella. A light, fruity and agreeable wine from the area near Verona.

Vino Bianco/White Wine

Frascati. A dry, reasonably-priced wine from the region near Rome.

Lacrima Christi. Just as memorable as the wine itself is its name, which means "the tears of Christ".

Orvieto. An excellent wine, dry and light, although it can sometimes be slightly sweet as well, from the Umbria region in central Italy.

Soave. This is produced in Umbria in a small town of the same name. It is one of Italy's best white wines, dry and crisp, and is perfect with fish and light meals.

Stufato di Manzo alla Romana

Roman Style Beef Stew

This old Roman recipe makes a perfect meal served with crusty Italian bread, red wine, and perhaps a small green salad. Make it ahead of time if you can, as it tastes even better the next day.

Ingredients	Regular	Metric
Beef, bottom round	2 lbs.	1 kg
Flour	4 oz.	125 ml
Salt	1/2 tsp.	2 ml
Pepper	1/4 tsp.	1 ml
Olive oil	2 tbsp.	30 ml
Bacon or pancetta slices, diced	2	2
Onion, chopped	1	1
Red wine	1 cup	250 ml
Beef stock	2 cups	500 ml
Bay leaves, crumbled	2	2
Carrots, cut up	3	3
Celery stalks, cut up	2	2
Mushrooms, halved	12	12
Tomato paste	2 tbsp.	30 ml

1. Cut the beef into bite-size pieces,and dredge in flour seasoned with salt and pepper.
2. Heat the oil in a large pot and cook the meat for 10 minutes, stirring occasionally, until well-browned all over.
3. Add the bacon and onion and cook for a few minutes more.
4. Add the remaining ingredients, lower the heat and cover the pot. Simmer for 1 hour, adding a little water if necessary, until meat is tender.

Serves 4-6

➤ *Using wine when slow-cooking meat not only adds a lovely taste, but acts as a natural tenderizer as well.*

Battuto

Battuto, also called soffrita, is an all-round base for soups and stews which originated in Rome. It consists of chopped vegetables and herbs, cooked in oil or butter. Chop medium fine:
  1 peeled onion
  1 peeled carrot
  1 peeled clove of garlic
  1 stalk celery
  2 tablespoons well-washed parsley
Cook and stir for 5 minutes in 2 oz. of oil or butter, then add whatever you want. Broth and additional vegetables for soup, meat and fish for stews. With battuto as a base, you can proceed in all kinds of different directions.

Fegato di Vitello con Funghi e Cipolla

Calf Liver with Mushrooms and Onions

Tender slices of calf liver with a colorful and tasty sauce of mushrooms, green peppers and onions cooked in tomato sauce and red wine.

Ingredients	Regular	Metric
Oil	3 tbsp.	45 ml
Butter	3 tbsp.	45 ml
Onion, sliced	1	1
Mushrooms, sliced	8	8
Green pepper, sliced	1	1
Tomato sauce	4 oz.	125 ml
Red wine	4 oz.	125 ml
Rosemary	Pinch	Pinch
Basil	1/4 tsp.	1 ml
Calf liver	1 lb.	500 g
Flour	4 oz.	125 ml
Salt	1/2 tsp.	2 ml
Pepper	Pinch	Pinch

1. Heat half the oil and butter in a frying pan and cook the onion, mushrooms, and green pepper for 5 minutes.
2. Add the tomato sauce, wine and seasonings, and simmer for 10 minutes.
3. Dredge the liver in flour seasoned with salt and pepper. Heat the rest of the oil and butter in another pan and, while the sauce is cooking, sauté the liver for about 2 minutes on each side.
4. Add the sauce to the liver, bring to a boil and then serve.

Serves 4-6

➤ *To prevent liver from shrinking up, take the pan off the heat just before adding the slices, then place back on the heat and continue to cook.*

Liver/Fegato

The organ meat most often eaten in North America is liver from beef. It's famous for iron, protein and vitamin A. Calf liver is the best and most tender, then comes baby beef liver, and lastly and least desirable, liver from the adult animal. If you have a choice, always buy calf liver, in spite of the price. It should have a pinkish-tan color, soft texture, and no odor.

Baby beef liver is a good second choice, and has a slightly darker color and firmer flesh. To soften it up, soak it in milk for about 30 minutes before cooking.

Liver has a membrane which should be removed before cooking to prevent the meat from curling up when the heat hits it. If the butcher hasn't already taken it away, do it yourself with a sharp knife.

Always wipe liver off with a damp cloth before cooking so that it will brown better, and never, never overcook it or it will become as tough as an old boot. No wonder some people don't like liver, when most of the time it has been cooked to death. If it's prepared properly, liver is not only a wonderful food for health and nutrition, but delicious and tender as well.

Fegato e Cipolle alla Venezia

Liver and Onions Venetian Style

This is an easy way to cook liver, and even people who don't like liver very much will enjoy this dish.

Ingredients	Regular	Metric
Calf liver	1 lb.	500 g
Flour	4 tbsp.	60 ml
Salt	1/2 tsp.	2 ml
Pepper	Pinch	Pinch
Oil	4 oz.	125 ml
Onions, sliced thinly	2	2
Garlic clove, minced	1	1

1. Slice liver into thin strips and dredge lightly in flour seasoned with salt and pepper.
2. Heat half the oil in a frying pan and cook the liver for 5 minutes over medium heat, then remove and keep warm.
3. Add the rest of the oil to the pan and cook the onions and garlic for 5 minutes until onion is soft and golden. Spoon onto liver and serve.

Serves 4

Animelle alla Panna

Sweetbreads with Cream

Sweetbreads have a very delicate flavor, and this white wine and cream sauce provides the perfect companion. Serve on top of your favorite pasta if you wish.

Ingredients	Regular	Metric
Veal sweetbreads	2 lbs.	1 kg
White vinegar	4 oz.	125 ml
Garlic cloves, chopped	2	2
Juice of 1 lemon		
Butter	2 tbsp.	30 ml

Oil	2 tbsp.	30 ml
White wine	4 oz.	125 ml
Heavy cream	6 oz.	200 ml
Salt	1/2 tsp.	2 ml
White pepper	Pinch	Pinch
Parsley, chopped	1 tbsp.	15 ml

1. Boil the sweetbreads for 8 minutes in a pot of water with the vinegar, garlic and lemon juice added.
2. Drain and rinse in cold water, then peel and cut into bite-size pieces.
3. Heat the butter and oil in a frying pan and cook the sweetbreads for 5 minutes.
4. Stir in the remaining ingredients and cook until the sauce has reduced by half, then serve.

Serves 4-6

VEAL
Vitello

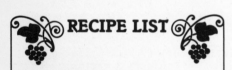
The Italian "kitchen" and tender veal go hand in hand, so it's important to know how to buy and cook it properly.

Top quality veal comes from calves 8-15 weeks old which have been fed entirely on milk. The meat is a light pinkish-white, and can usually be found at Italian markets or other good butcher shops, but since it is quite expensive, much of the veal available is from older calves and has a slightly darker meat. We call this baby beef *vitellone*.

Since veal comes from a young animal, it has little fat and no marbling, so it should be cooked for as short a time as possible or else it will get dry and tough. It is best pounded thin and cooked quickly, as in *scaloppine*, or braised and cooked in liquid.

Veal cutlets, scaloppine and paillard all come from the leg, as does the meat for Ossobucco, but if you want the very best cuts, ask for the meat from the inside of the leg, or *fesa di vitello*.

Piccata di Vitello alla Lombarda

Veal Scaloppine Lombardy Style

This dish comes from the Lombardy region of Italy—the flat plains which surround Milan. The green and red peppers, mushrooms, and tomatoes make it a colorful as well as tasty dish.

Ingredients	Regular	Metric
Veal	1 lb.	500 g
Flour	4 oz.	125 ml
Salt	1/2 tsp.	2 ml
Pepper	Pinch	Pinch
Olive oil	2 tbsp.	30 ml
Butter	2 tbsp.	30 ml
Green pepper, sliced	1	1
Red pepper, sliced	1	1
Garlic clove, chopped	1	1
Mushrooms, sliced	8	8
Tomatoes, peeled and chopped	2	2
White wine	4 oz.	125 ml
Parsley, chopped	2 tbsp.	30 ml
Olives, chopped	4 oz.	125 ml

1. Cut the veal into 8 pieces and pound very thin, then dredge lightly in flour seasoned with salt and pepper.
2. Heat the oil and butter in a large frying pan and cook the veal very quickly for 1 minute each side. Remove and keep warm.
3. Add more oil to the pan if necessary, and cook the peppers, garlic, onion and mushrooms for 5 minutes.
4. Add the tomatoes and wine, and simmer for 5 minutes more. Stir in the parsley and pour the sauce over the veal, then serve with the olives sprinkled on top.

Serves 4-6

▶ *Never cook scaloppine too long or the meat will be tough. Pound veal cutlets very thinly, then cook quickly in oil and butter – one minute on each side should be enough. Watch for the red juices to come to the surface of the meat, and then turn over.*

Scaloppine di Vitello Piccata

Veal with Lemon

Veal cutlets, pounded into thin piccata or scaloppine, are cooked quickly in butter, then seasoned gently with parsley and lemon. Fast, easy—and delicious.

Ingredients	Regular	Metric
Veal cutlets	1 lb.	500 g
Flour	4 tbsp.	60 ml
Salt	1/2 tsp.	2 ml
Pepper	Pinch	Pinch
Butter	2 tbsp.	30 ml
Oil	2 tbsp.	30 ml
Parsley, chopped	2 tbsp.	30 ml
Juice of 1 lemon		

1. Cut the meat into 8 pieces and pound into thin scaloppine, then dredge lightly in flour seasoned with salt and pepper.
2. Heat the butter and oil in a large frying pan, and cook the veal for 1 minute on each side.
3. Add the parsley and lemon juice to the pan and coat the veal thoroughly, then serve immediately.

Serves 4-6

➤ *When you only want to use a little bit of lemon juice, prick the end of a lemon with a fork, squeeze out a few drops of juice, then put the lemon back in the refrigerator to use later.*

Preparing Veal Scaloppine

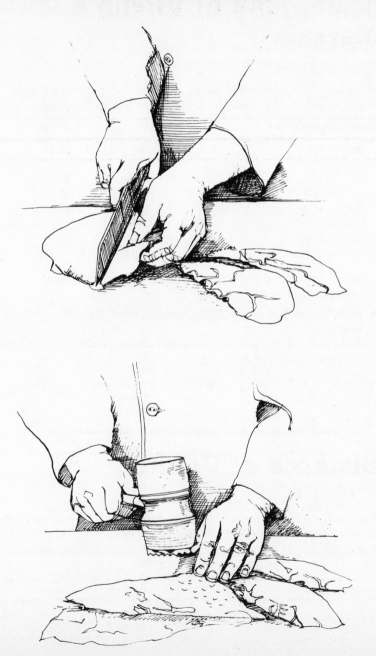

1. Cutting across the grain of the meat, slice off cutlets about $1/2''$ thickness.

2. Lay the cutlet flat on a board and place a piece of plastic wrap over the top. Now lightly pound with a meat hammer until it becomes the thickness you prefer.

Scaloppine di Vitello alla Marsala

Veal Scaloppine with Marsala Wine

This should be cooked and served very quickly or the veal will get tough. So pronto!—in and out of the pan and onto the plate.

Ingredients	Regular	Metric
Veal cutlets	4	4
Flour	4 oz.	125 ml
Salt	1 tsp.	5 ml
Pepper	Pinch	Pinch
Butter	2 tbsp.	30 ml
Marsala wine	4 oz.	125 ml
Chicken stock	2 oz.	50 ml
Parsley, chopped	1 tbsp.	30 ml

1. Pound the cutlets into thin scaloppine, then dredge lightly in flour seasoned with salt and pepper.
2. Heat the butter in a large frying pan and cook for 1 minute on each side.
3. Add the wine, stock and parsley and simmer for 3 minutes. Serve with the sauce on top.

Serves 4

Marsala

Marsala is the most popular of the Italian fortified wines, and Sicily's most famous export. It has been made on that island for literally thousands of years, in a method very similar to the making of sherry in Spain, and usually has an alcoholic content of between 17-19%. Although sugar content varies, it is the sweet variety which is liked best after dinner, and its distinctive almond-cherry flavor makes it a popular wine to cook with.

Bistecca di Vitello

Veal Paillard

A paillard is a cut of meat which is pounded, but not quite as thinly as scaloppine. Veal paillard, veal cooked in white wine and butter, is one of the simplest veal dishes there is. Be careful not to overcook it—only one minute on each side.

Ingredients	Regular	Metric
Veal cutlets, inside cut	4-6 oz. each	4-200 g each
Butter, melted	4 tbsp.	60 ml
Crushed peppercorns	1 tbsp.	15 ml
Salt	1/2 tsp.	2 ml

"Don't forget that your guests should be happy, so if something goes wrong in the kitchen, just try to make the best of it and not get upset. Food tastes better with a smile."

Sage	1 tbsp.	15 ml
Oil	2 tbsp.	30 ml
White wine	4 oz.	125 ml
Lemon wedges	8	8

1. Pound cutlets until they are $1/4$"/$1/2$ cm thick, then coat with butter, pepper, salt and sage.
2. Heat oil in a large frying pan and cook veal for 1 minute each side. Remove to heated serving platter.
3. Add wine to the pan and let it reduce for several minutes, then pour the sauce over the veal and serve with lemon wedges.

Serves 4

Saltimbocca

Veal with Ham and Sage

This easily prepared and well-known dish dates back to Roman times. The literal translation of "saltimbocca" is "jump into the mouth" which should give you a good idea how tasty it is.

Ingredients	Regular	Metric
Veal cutlets	8	8
Sage	1 tsp.	5 ml
Pepper	Pinch	Pinch
Prosciutto or ham slices	8	8
Butter	2 tbsp.	30 ml
Oil	2 tbsp.	30 ml
White wine	4 oz.	125 ml

1. Pound the cutlets into thin scaloppine, then sprinkle each piece with sage and pepper and put a slice of ham on top. Press the edges together firmly.
2. Heat the butter and oil in a large frying pan and cook the meat for 2-3 minutes on each side, until nicely browned all over.
3. Remove to a heated platter and add the wine to the pan. Let it boil up for 1 minute, then pour over the meat and serve.

Serves 4-6

Sage/Salvia

Sage is a herb native to the Mediterranean, and has many uses in Italian cooking – in stuffings, sausages, and cheeses – but none so famous as in *saltimbocca*.

It should never be cooked too long at high temperatures, though, or its taste will change and become camphorous.

Piccata di Vitello con Peperoni Verde

Veal Piccata with Green Peppers

Thin slices of veal, lightly coated in flour and beaten egg, and served in a delicately spiced sauce of green peppers and white wine.

Ingredients	Regular	Metric
Veal, inside cut	1 lb.	500 g
Flour	3 tbsp.	45 ml
Salt	1/2 tsp.	2 ml
Pepper	Pinch	Pinch
Oregano	1/2 tsp.	2 ml
Eggs, beaten	2	2
Oil	2 tbsp.	30 ml
Butter	2 tbsp.	30 ml
Green peppers	2	2
Garlic clove, minced	1	1
White wine	4 oz.	125 ml
Parsley, chopped	1 tbsp.	30 ml

1. Cut the veal into 8 pieces and pound into thin scaloppine. Dredge lightly in flour seasoned with salt, pepper and oregano, then dip in beaten egg.
2. Heat oil and butter in a large frying pan and cook meat for 2 minutes each side, then remove and keep warm.
3. Slice green peppers thinly and add to the pan with the garlic. Cook and stir for 5 minutes, then add the wine and cook another 3-5 minutes.
4. Pour the sauce over the veal and serve sprinkled with chopped parsley.

Serves 4-6

► *Always cook veal scaloppine quickly in a hot pan, and pour the sauce on just before serving. If you try to cook the meat with the sauce, it will become tough.*

Imoltini di Vitello con Formaggio

Veal Cutlets Stuffed with Cheese

In this recipe, veal cutlets are stuffed with grated cheeses, then cooked in butter and served with a wine sauce.

Ingredients	Regular	Metric
Veal cutlets	4	4
Mozzarella cheese, grated	4 oz.	125 ml
Parmesan cheese, grated	2 oz.	50 ml
Egg, beaten	1	1
Sage	1 tsp.	5 ml
Flour	4 oz.	125 ml
Salt	1/2 tsp.	2 ml
Pepper	Pinch	Pinch
Butter	4 tbsp.	60 ml
White wine	2 oz.	50 ml
Sweet vermouth	2 oz.	50 ml

1. Make pockets in the veal by cutting into one side with a sharp knife, and going almost over to the other side, then slicing through lengthwise.
2. Combine the cheeses, egg and sage, and stuff the mixture inside the pockets.
3. Dredge the veal lightly in flour seasoned with salt and pepper.
4. Heat the butter in a large frying pan, then cook the veal until it is browned on both sides.
5. Add the wine and vermouth, and cook, covered, for 10 minutes.
6. Remove cutlets to a heated serving platter and reduce the sauce for several minutes, then pour over the veal and serve.

Serves 4

Mozzarella

Mozzarella is a melting cheese like fontina and is used in many Italian recipes like lasagne and pizza. It has a stringy texture when melted which gives it a nice "bite", but is very mild and pleasant tasting.

Vitello con Melanzana Indorare

Veal with Eggplant and Cheese

"Indorare" is the word used to describe the method of coating food in flour and beaten egg, and then frying. Generally, it is used for meats, but in this recipe, it's the way the eggplant and tomato slices are cooked.

Ingredients	Regular	Metric
Veal cutlets	6	6
Flour	4 oz.	125 ml
Salt	1/2 tsp.	2 ml
Pepper	Pinch	Pinch
Olive oil	4 oz.	125 ml
Garlic cloves, chopped	2	2
Eggs, beaten	2	2
Thin eggplant slices	6	6
Tomato slices	6	6
Mozzarella cheese slices	6	6
Red wine	4 oz.	125 ml
Tomato sauce	1 cup	250 ml
Oregano	Pinch	Pinch
Basil	Pinch	Pinch
Parsley, chopped	1 tbsp.	15 ml

► *To remove excess moisture and bitterness from eggplant, place slices in a colander, and sprinkle them with salt. Cover with a plate with a five pound weight on top – two heavy cans of something are fine – and leave for twenty minutes, then rinse. This method is also very good for making cucumber slices completely "burpless".*

1. Pound the veal into thin scaloppine and dredge lightly in flour seasoned with salt and pepper.
2. Heat half the oil in a large frying pan and add the garlic, then cook the veal for 1 minute on each side. Remove and drain.
3. Dip the eggplant and tomato slices in the flour, then in the beaten egg. Heat the rest of the oil in the pan and cook the slices for 1 minute on each side. Remove and drain.
4. Pour off excess oil, then place veal back in the pan with a slice of eggplant, a slice of tomato and a slice of mozzarella on top of each piece. Add wine, tomato sauce and seasonings, and simmer, covered, for 5 minutes. Sprinkle with parsley and serve with the sauce.

Serves 4-6

Ossobucco Milanese

Stewed Shank of Veal

Have your butcher cut the center of the shank into 2"/5 cm thick pieces when you buy it. The name literally means "bone with a hole", and the marrow adds a special flavor. You can enjoy it by picking it out of the center of the bone and eating it slowly—very tasty.

Ingredients	Regular	Metric
Veal shank	2 lbs.	1 kg
Flour	4 tbsp.	60 ml
Salt	1/2 tsp.	2 ml
Pepper	Pinch	Pinch
Oil	4 tbsp.	60 ml
Onion, chopped	1	1
Garlic cloves, chopped	2	2
Celery stalk, diced	1	1
Carrot, sliced	1	1
Chicken stock	1 cup	250 ml
White wine	6 oz.	200 ml
Tomatoes, peeled and chopped	1 cup	250 ml
Orange peel, grated	1 tbsp.	15 ml
Tomato paste	4 tbsp.	60 ml

1. Preheat oven to 350°F./180°C.
2. Dredge the veal pieces in flour seasoned with salt and pepper.
3. Heat the oil in a large frying pan and cook the veal until brown all over, then remove to a baking dish.
4. Put the onion, garlic, celery and carrot into the pan, and cook for 5 minutes, then add remaining ingredients and simmer for 3 minutes before pouring over the veal.
5. Cook in the oven for 2 hours, then serve with a large dish of risotto.

Serves 4-6

▶ *Try to arrange the bones in Ossobucco upright in the pan so that the marrow doesn't fall out.*

Steam Roasting

This is a method of roasting I developed which is wonderful for cooking all kinds of meat and fowl.

First of all, I heat the oven to a high temperature at the beginning. This seals in the juices, and makes the meat lovely and crisp on the outside.

Then I lower the temperature about 100°F., add various liquids to the pan, and continue roasting until the meat is just right. Since the temperature is still fairly high, the meat doesn't dry out from overcooking, it's done much more quickly, and the liquids in the bottom of the pan provide enough moisture to keep the texture juicy and tender. They also provide pan drippings which make a wonderful tasting gravy. I cook lamb, pork, and beef roasts this way, plus chicken and turkey.

If you're using this technique for the first time, you may want to use a meat thermometer until you get used to the timing, but I guarantee that you will love this method and never use any other, once you have tried it.

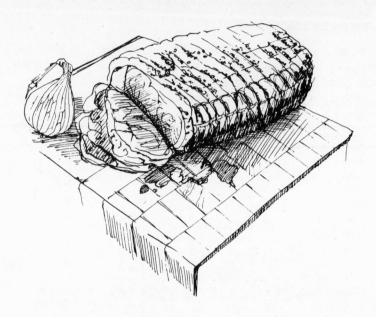

Vitello al Forno

Oven Roasted Veal

A veal roast made even more tender and juicy cooked with my special method of steam-roasting.

Ingredients	Regular	Metric
Shoulder of veal, rolled and tied	3 lb.	1 1/2 kg
Bacon or pancetta slices	4	4
Salt	1 tsp.	5 ml
Pepper	Pinch	Pinch
Rosemary	1 tsp.	5 ml
Thyme	1 tsp.	5 ml
Celery stalk, chopped	1	1
Onion, halved	1	1
Carrot, sliced	1	1
White vinegar	4 oz.	125 ml

White wine	4 oz.	125 ml
Water	1 cup	250 ml
Lemon, juice and peel	1	1

1. Preheat oven to 475°F./240°C.
2. Place meat in roasting pan and lay the bacon slices on top, then sprinkle with seasonings.
3. Cook in the oven for 45 minutes, remove and lower the heat to 375°F./190°C. Let pan cool slightly and then add the remaining ingredients.
4. Place back in oven and cook for another 60 minutes. Remove roast and let stand for 10 minutes before slicing to let the juices settle. Strain the pan liquids and use as gravy.

Serves 6

Costolette di Vitello Marinato

Broiled Veal Chops with Mint

Veal chops are marinated in mint and orange juice, and then broiled. Don't forget to baste the meat with the marinade while barbecueing.

Ingredients	Regular	Metric
Veal chops	6-6 oz. each.	6-200 g each
Oil	4 tbsp.	60 ml
Sherry or vermouth	4 oz.	125 ml
Mint flakes	2 tbsp.	30 ml
Parsley, chopped	2 tbsp.	30 ml
Paprika	1 tbsp.	15 ml
Orange juice	1 cup.	250 ml
Salt	1 tsp.	5 ml
Pepper	Pinch	Pinch

1. Combine ingredients and marinate the veal for 1-2 hours.
2. Place chops 6"/15 cm beneath heated broiler, or on the barbecue, and cook for 6 minutes each side basting with the marinade.

Serves 4-6

> ➤ *Although mint is most commonly associated with lamb, its pungent, tingling flavor makes it a favorite companion for many foods. Combined with the acidic sweetness of orange juice, it makes a wonderful marinade for veal chops — especially for summer barbecues.*

Provolone

Provolone cheese is one of the finest eating cheeses in Italy, and is available *dolce* or *piccante* – the piccante being stronger. It is good eaten fresh, but is also excellent as a grated cheese when it goes a bit stale.

Filetto di Vitello Stravaganza

Fillet of Veal Extravaganza

Tender medallions of veal in a rich cream sauce topped with provolone cheese. A beautiful dish to surprise and spoil some special guests.

Ingredients	Regular	Metric
Fillet of veal	2 lbs.	1 kg
Flour	4 oz.	125 ml
Butter	2 tbsp.	30 ml
Oil	2 tbsp.	30 ml
Green onions, chopped	4	4
Tomatoes, peeled and chopped	2	2
Curry powder	1 tsp.	5 ml
Sage	1/2 tsp.	2 ml
Anchovies, chopped	4	4
Juice of 2 lemons		
White wine	2 oz.	50 ml
Brandy	2 oz.	50 ml
Strega liqueur	1 oz.	25 ml
Beef broth	2 oz.	50 ml
Heavy cream	6 oz.	200 ml
Salt	1/2 tsp.	2 ml
Pepper	Pinch	Pinch
Provolone cheese slices	6 slices	6 slices
Parsley, chopped	2 tbsp.	30 ml

1. Cut veal into 1"/2 cm medallions and dredge lightly with flour.
2. Heat oil and butter in a large frying pan and cook the veal for 2 minutes on each side, then add the green onions and cook 1 minute more.
3. Add the next 12 ingredients and simmer for 10 minutes, or until liquid is reduced by half.
4. Top with cheese slices and cover. When cheese has melted, sprinkle with parsley and serve.

Serves 4-6

Umido Bianco di Vitello

Veal Stew in White Wine

Veal is a tender meat to start out with so you don't have to "stew" this dish as much as you would other meats.

Ingredients	Regular	Metric
Veal shoulder	1 lb.	500 g
Flour	4 oz.	125 ml
Salt	1/2 tsp.	2 ml
Pepper	Pinch	Pinch
Bacon or pancetta slices, diced	2	2
Onion, chopped	1	1
Celery stalks, chopped	2	2
Carrot, diced	1	1
Garlic clove, chopped	1	1
Chicken stock	4 oz.	125 ml
White wine	4 oz.	125 ml
Bay leaf, crumbled	1	1
Tarragon	Pinch	Pinch
Parsley, chopped	1 tbsp.	15 ml

1. Cut the veal into bite-size pieces and dredge lightly in flour seasoned with salt and pepper.
2. Cook the bacon in a large pot until the fat is reduced, then add the veal cubes. Cook and stir until brown all over.
3. Add the vegetables and garlic, and cook for another 10 minutes, then add the stock, wine, bay leaf and tarragon. Cover and simmer gently for 30 minutes.
4. When meat is tender, check seasonings and stir in parsley just before serving.

Serves 4-6

Bayleaf/Laura

Bayleaves come from the evergreen Laurel tree. In Greek and Roman times, the fresh boughs from these trees were woven into head wreaths for victors in games and war, and for great intellectual achievement. Someone who didn't go out and try to better former efforts was said to be "resting on their laurels".

The leaves dry well, and retain their flavor for quite a long time. Once they get brittle, though, they're not much good. Use in marinades, soups, stews, and other long-cooking dishes.

Vitello Farcito

Stuffed Veal Roll

When you slice the finished veal roll crossways, the servings have a pinwheel effect which makes a very nice presentation on the plate.

Ingredients	Regular	Metric
Veal flank	2 lbs.	1 kg
Breadcrumbs	4 oz.	125 ml
Egg, lightly beaten	1	1
Mushrooms, chopped finely	8	8
Garlic powder	1 tsp.	5 ml
Sage	1 tsp.	5 ml
Anchovy fillets, chopped	6	6
Flour	2 tbsp.	30 ml
Salt	1/2 tsp.	2 ml
Pepper	Pinch	Pinch
Parsley, chopped	2 tbsp.	30 ml
Chicken stock	4 oz.	125 ml
White wine	2 oz.	50 ml

1. Preheat the oven to 450°F./230°C.
2. Pound the veal until flattened into a large rectangular shape. Combine the next 10 ingredients and spread on the veal.
3. Roll up the veal, jelly-roll fashion, and tie securely with string.
4. Put roll in a roasting pan and cook in the oven for 1 hour, then lower the heat to 350°F./180°C add the liquids to the pan, and cook another 30 minutes.
5. Remove veal to heated serving platter, slice crossways, and serve.

Serves 4-6

► *Whenever you use anchovies in a recipe, taste the dish carefully before adding extra salt.*

Costolette di Vitello Saporite

Veal Chops with Horseradish Sauce

In Italian, horseradish is "radica forte" which literally means strong roots, so be very careful not to use too much or you won't be able to taste the veal.

Ingredients	Regular	Metric
Oil	4 tbsp.	60 ml
Veal chops	6-4 oz. each.	6-125 g each
Flour	4 tbsp.	60 ml
Salt	1/2 tsp.	2 ml
Pepper	Pinch	Pinch
Butter	4 tbsp.	60 ml
Green onions, chopped	4	4
Prepared horseradish	3 tbsp.	45 ml
White wine	4 oz.	125 ml
Chicken stock	4 oz.	125 ml
Heavy cream	4 oz.	125 ml
Sage	Pinch	Pinch

1. Heat oil in a large frying pan.
2. Dredge chops lightly in flour seasoned with salt and pepper, and cook for 4 minutes on each side. Remove and keep warm.
3. Melt butter in the same pan and cook the onions for 1 minute, then add the other ingredients and simmer until sauce is reduced by half.
4. Pour sauce over veal and serve immediately.

Serves 4-6

PORK
Maiale

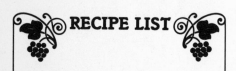
Pork has always been a popular meat, because of its conven-
ience and wonderful taste when cured or air-dried. Even now
that refrigeration is taken for granted in many countries, cured
meat still accounts for about two-thirds of all the pork eaten, and
in Italy, different types of sausages and salt-cured pork add de-
liciously to the cuisine in many ways.

If you are buying fresh pork, however, look for light-colored
meat with firm white fat. The more color the flesh has, the older
the animal was, and the tougher the meat will be. Fresh pork is
at its best cooked quickly in a frying pan, or roasted in the oven.
The loin is the most desirable of the choice cuts. You can get
chops from any part of this section, but the center is where you
find the best roasts and, of course, the juicy pork tenderloin.

Since pork should be cooked until it is well-done, it is most
important that it should never be allowed to dry out, and my
recipes make sure that the meat will always be moist and tender.

Braciola di Maiale

Stuffed Rolls of Pork Tenderloin

You can vary this recipe by making "little bundles". Just pound out smaller slices of pork, roll them up with the stuffing and secure with toothpicks. The bundles make nice individual servings.

Ingredients	Regular	Metric
Pork tenderloin fillets	2-1 lb. each	2-500 g each
Chestnuts, drained	1 small can	1 small can
Grapes	4 oz.	125 g
Apples, peeled and chopped	2	2
Breadcrumbs	1/2 cup	125 ml
Parsley, chopped	1 tbsp.	15 ml
Flour	2 tbsp.	30 ml
White wine	6 oz.	200 ml
White vinegar	2 oz.	50 ml

1. Preheat oven to 450°F./230°C.
2. Slice the fillets almost all the way through lengthwise, then spread them open so they are lying flat.
3. Place plastic wrap over the meat and pound it until it is $^{1}/_{2}$"/1 cm thick all over.
4. Mix the chestnuts, grapes, apples, breadcrumbs and parsley together, and put half on each fillet, down the middle lengthwise.
5. Roll the meat over and around the stuffing, then wrap in aluminum foil and seal the edges.
6. Place fillets in a baking dish with a little water on the bottom and cook for 45 minutes, then turn the heat down to 350°F./180°C and pour the wine and vinegar into the pan. Cook for another 45-60 minutes.
7. Remove foil and slice meat crossways. Place on a heated platter and pour the sauce on top.

Serves 4-6

Chestnut/Caldarrosti

Chestnuts are excellent served with pork. Be sure to get the sweet or Spanish chestnut which has been cultivated in the Mediterranean region for thousands of years.

Chestnuts can be roasted, boiled, steamed, grilled, and then mashed. In many recipes, canned chestnuts are just fine.

► *Here's the method for cooking and mashing fresh chestnuts. When you buy them, ask for cooking chestnuts, then slit each one with a sharp knife and cover with water. Bring to a boil and cook for 30 minutes until the shells are even more split and the meat is soft. Remove to cold water, and when you can handle them, peel and mash. Use in stuffings, sweets and sauces.*

Filetto di Maiale alla Canadese

Pork Tenderloin with Apple

Pork and apples are a traditional combination, and since Canada is famous for its fine apples, I named this dish "Canadese". If your region also has good apples, then name this recipe for your home.

> ➤ *Always choose chops and cutlets from the loin or best end of neck, and be sure that all the fat is drained away from the pan before other ingredients are added. Pork is wonderful with apples, with apple cider, or with applesauce.*

Ingredients	Regular	Metric
Pork tenderloin	2 lbs.	1 kg
Flour	2 tbsp.	30 ml
Oil	2 tbsp.	30 ml
Butter	2 tbsp.	30 ml
Onion, sliced	1	1
Mushrooms, sliced	6	6
Green pepper, sliced	1	1
Apple, cored and sliced	1	1
Basil	Pinch	Pinch
Curry powder	1 tsp.	5 ml
Oregano	Pinch	Pinch
Salt	1/2 tsp.	2 ml
Pepper	Pinch	Pinch
Tomato paste	2 tbsp.	30 ml
Beef stock or consommé	1 cup	250 ml
Red wine	4 oz.	125 ml

1. Cut pork into $1/2$"/1 cm slices and dredge lightly with flour.
2. Heat oil and butter in a large frying pan and cook pork for 3 minutes on each side.
3. Add onion, mushrooms, green pepper, apple and seasonings, then cook and stir for 5 minutes.
4. Add tomato paste and liquids, and simmer for 10 minutes.
5. Sprinkle with a little chopped parsley if you like, and serve with egg noodles.

Serves 6

Cotolette di Maiale Ripiene

Pork Cutlets Stuffed with Ham and Cheese

The happy combination of pork, prosciutto and cheese makes this a tasty dish, but be careful to seal the edges of the pork carefully so that none of the delicious cheese leaks out.

Ingredients	Regular	Metric
Pork cutlets	4	4
Prosciutto slices	4	4
Mozzarella cheese slices	4	4
Flour	4 oz.	125 ml
Salt	1/2 tsp.	2 ml
Pepper	Pinch	Pinch
Eggs, beaten	2	2
Cream or milk	2 oz.	50 ml
Fine breadcrumbs	1 cup.	250 ml
Butter	2 tbsp.	30 ml
Oil	2 tbsp.	30 ml
White wine	4 oz.	125 ml
Tomato sauce	4 oz.	125 ml

1. Preheat oven to 350°F./180°C.
2. Pound the pork cutlets until very thin, then put a slice of prosciutto and a slice of cheese on each one. Fold the meat over and pound the edges to seal.
3. Season the flour with salt and pepper and dredge the pork lightly.
4. Mix the eggs and cream together and dip the dredged pork into this liquid, then pat in the breadcrumbs until well-coated.
5. Heat the oil and butter in a large frying pan and cook the pork for 5 minutes on each side. Put in a baking dish and cover with the wine and tomato sauce. Cook in the oven for 15 minutes, then serve with the sauce poured on top.

Serves 4

Costolette di Maiale al Pomodoro

Pork Chops in Tomatoes

Pork chops, braised and cooked slowly in a sauce of wine and tomatoes, make a tender and flavorful dish.

Ingredients	Regular	Metric
Oil	2 tbsp.	30 ml
Pork chops	8-4 oz. each.	8-125 g. each
Onion, sliced thinly	1	1
Garlic cloves, minced	3	3
Red wine	4 oz.	125 ml
Tomatoes, peeled and chopped	3	3
Tomato paste	2 tbsp.	30 ml
Red wine vinegar	2 oz.	50 ml
Oregano	Pinch	Pinch
Salt	1/2 tsp.	2 ml
Pepper	Pinch	Pinch
Parsley	1 tbsp.	15 ml

1. Heat the oil in a large frying pan and fry the chops until well-browned on both sides.
2. Add the onion and garlic and cook for another 5 minutes.
3. Add remaining ingredients, cover and simmer for 20 minutes, then remove the chops to a heated platter and serve with the sauce on top.

Serves 4-6

Costatine di Maiale Agra Dolce

Sweet and Sour Spareribs

This is also very good for a summer barbecue. Marinate the ribs in the sauce, and then use to baste as the ribs cook.

Ingredients	Regular	Metric
Garlic cloves, minced	2	2
Salt	1 tsp.	5 ml

> ➤ *If you've put too much salt in a recipe, a small pinch of sugar will correct it.*

> ➤ *The Pharoahs thought so much of garlic that they used to be buried with it so they could take it into the afterworld with them.*

Pepper	1/2 tsp.	2 ml
Honey	6 oz.	200 ml
Red wine vinegar	2 oz.	50 ml
Juice of 1 lemon		
Pork back ribs	4 lbs.	2 kg

1. Mix the first 6 ingredients together in a bowl, and let stand for 1 hour.
2. Cut the ribs into 4-rib sections, and place in a roasting pan. Broil for 5 minutes on each side.
3. Drain off fat, then pour the sauce over the ribs and cook in a preheated 400°F./200°C oven for 30 minutes, basting occasionally. Serve with the sauce poured over the ribs.

Serves 4-6

Salsiccie Fritti

Sausage with Sweet Red Peppers and Onion

Any kind of sausage is good cooked this way, whether it's plain or spicy. Use the sausage you make yourself, or whatever you choose to buy from a good Italian butcher.

Ingredients	Regular	Metric
Sausage	2 lbs.	2 kg
Oil	2 oz.	50 ml
Sweet red peppers, sliced	3	3
Onion, sliced	1	1
Basil	Pinch	Pinch
Oregano	Pinch	Pinch
Garlic clove, minced	1	1
Salt	1/2 tsp.	2 ml
Pepper	Pinch	Pinch

1. Put the sausage in a large frying pan with $1/2$"/1 cm of water in the bottom. Cover and cook over medium heat until the water has evaporated.
2. Add the oil and fry until sausage has browned all over. Remove and keep warm.
3. Place the peppers, onion and seasonings in the pan and cook for 5 minutes, then put sausages back in. Cook for 5 more minutes, then place on a heated platter and serve.

Serves 4-6

Sausages/Salsiccie

Italians make some of the finest pork sausage in the world, and much of it is made at home. These are some of the best-known types.

Abruzzi. These sausages are made from finely ground pork, spices, and sometimes red wine, then cured and air-dried.

Allesandri. These are hard, dry and spicy.

Calabrian. Made with coarsely ground pork, spices, and hot chili peppers.

Soprassate. A general term for salami, which literally means "pressed together".

Cacciatori. Sausages which come in small sizes.

1. Pass the pork, and other meats if you wish, through the meat grinder. Pass through again if you do not want a coarse sausage. Now mix the minced meat with your spices.

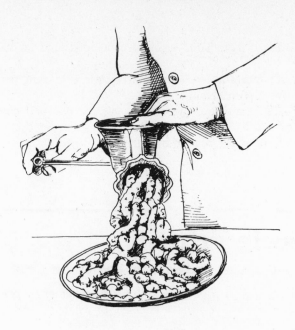

2. Place the pork intestine over the top of the funnel attachment on your meat grinder.

3. Fill the meat casing by holding the casing with one hand, making sure it is tightly packed with meat and has no air spots.

4. Tie up the ends of the casing and twist into links.

Fennel

Salsiccie Calabrese

Calabrian Sausage

This spicy sausage is like the salsiccie they make at home in Calabria. It's a lot of fun to make, especially if you like working with your hands, and it tastes so good that it's well worth the effort.

Ingredients	Regular	Metric
Pork shoulder	4 lbs.	2 kg
Salt	4 tbsp.	60 ml
Ground black pepper	4 tbsp.	60 ml
Paprika	4 tbsp.	60 ml
Fennel, chopped	1 tbsp.	15 ml
Chili peppers	2 tbsp.	30 ml
Pork intestines	2	2

1. Medium grind pork and put in a bowl with the seasonings. Mix well with the hands until a piece sticks to your palm when you hold your hands upside down.
2. Take the cutting blades out of the grinder, and put on the funnel attachment.
3. Slide one end of the intestine over the mouth of the funnel, and then work it back over the attachment until just the other end is left hanging. Tie this end off.
4. Place the pork mixture back in the machine and turn the handle slowly until the meat starts to fill the casing. Ease the mixture down the casing with your other hand to make sure that the meat is firmly packed. If any air gets trapped, poke casing to get it out.
5. When casing is full, tie off the other end and twist every 6"/15 cm to make individual links.

Makes 12-16 links

Salsiccie e Fagioli

Sausage and Beans

This is a very old generic Italian recipe, and probably the inspiration for "pork and beans".

Ingredients	Regular	Metric
Olive oil	3 tbsp.	45 ml
Sausage links	2 lbs.	2 kg
Onion, chopped	1	1
Garlic cloves, chopped	2	2
Celery stalk, chopped	1	1
Tomato sauce	1 cup	250 ml
Tomato paste	2 tbsp.	30 ml
Kidney or Romano beans, drained	19 oz. can	575 ml can
Basil	Pinch	Pinch
Salt	1/2 tsp.	2 ml
Pepper	Pinch	Pinch

➤ *Beans are a natural food to serve with pork all over the world, as their mealiness absorbs any of the fat.*

1. Heat oil in a large pot. Cut sausage into bite-size pieces and add to the pot with the onion, garlic and celery, then cook and stir for 5 minutes.
2. Add the tomato sauce and paste, and cook until the liquid has reduced by half.
3. Add the beans and seasonings and simmer for 5 minutes. Serve in individual bowls.

Serves 4

LAMB
Agnello

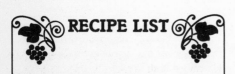
Lamb is the food of Spring, and tender spring lamb, associated with Easter and rebirth, has always been the most desirable. These youngsters, born in February and March, become available at the beginning of April and throughout the summer. Nowadays, young lamb can be obtained all year long, and so the term "spring lamb" is not strictly accurate, although it is still used to describe lamb which is young and small.

There are many cuts of lamb, but the most popular is the leg. The best meat comes from a leg weighing 4-5 pounds, but a leg from an older lamb can go up to 8 pounds. Sometimes butchers will sell half a leg at a time, with the shank being the best part. Often the lamb will come frozen, so be sure to defrost it very slowly in the refrigerator for the finest taste.

It used to be the fashion to cook lamb until it was really well-done, then suddenly everyone wanted it very rare, but now things have evened out and most people like their lamb cooked until it is just a delicate pink inside. If this is the way you like it, cook the meat at a lower temperature (325°F.) for a shorter period of time, 12-15 minutes per pound.

One of the reasons some people say they don't like lamb is that when it was overcooked, it developed a strong odor. This was from the fat. Lamb fat melts more slowly than the fats on other meats, but when it finally does, it gives the meat a strong flavor and smells up the kitchen, so people started cooking lamb very rare to avoid this.

But the way I have of roasting a leg of lamb gives you a meat that is tender and juicy, and done just enough so that it smells delicious, tastes beautiful, and is easier to digest than very rare lamb. Magnifico!

Abbachio Arrosto alla Romana

Roman Style Roast Lamb

This ancient recipe dates back to Roman times, and is a fine example of the fact that if something is good enough, it will last. Leg of lamb is roasted with anchovies, garlic and capers, then cooked to complete tenderness in a seasoned wine sauce.

Ingredients	Regular	Metric
Leg of lamb	5 lbs.	2 1/2 kg
Anchovy fillets, cut up	6	6
Garlic cloves, halved	3	3
Capers	2 tbsp.	30 ml
Rosemary	1 tbsp.	15 ml
Mint flakes	1 tbsp.	15 ml
Dry mustard	1 tbsp.	15 ml
Salt	1 tsp.	5 ml
Pepper	Pinch	Pinch
Juice of 1 lemon		
Red wine	4 oz.	125 ml
Wine vinegar	4 oz.	125 ml

1. Preheat oven to 375°F./190°C.
2. Make small cuts all over the lamb and insert the anchovies, garlic and capers.
3. Rub seasonings over the lamb and squeeze lemon juice on top.
4. Cook in the oven for 2 hours, then reduce heat to 325°F./160°C.
5. Add liquids to the pan and cook for another hour. Remove and let stand for several minutes, then carve and serve.
6. Strain pan juices and pour over slices.

Serves 6-8

Caper/Capperi

Capers are the unopened flower buds of the caper bush which grows wild in Mediterranean regions. After the buds are picked, they are dried and then pickled in vinegar.

Their tart quality makes them go well with fish and meat — also eggplant, tomato and olives. Since they last for such a long time, they are handy to keep in the refrigerator for that extra little touch when you need it.

Abbachio in Padella

Spring Lamb Sauté

If you enjoy lamb, but would like a change from roasting or broiling, try this simple method of preparation. The recipe is very old, and traditionally calls only for fresh spring lamb.

Ingredients	Regular	Metric
Oil	2 tbsp.	30 ml
Salt pork or bacon, chopped	4 oz.	125 ml
Leg of lamb	4 lb.	2 kg
Onion, sliced	1	1
Garlic cloves, chopped	2	2
Anchovy fillets, chopped	4	4
White wine	4 oz.	125 ml
White wine vinegar	2 oz.	50 ml
Stock or water	4 oz.	125 ml
Bay leaves	2	2
Rosemary	2 tbsp.	30 ml
Dried mint	Pinch	Pinch
Parsley, chopped	1 tbsp.	15 ml

1. Heat the oil in a large pot, and cook the salt pork and lamb for 10 minutes until meat is browned all over.
2. Add onion and garlic and cook for another 5 minutes.
3. Add all the other ingredients, except the parsley, and bring to a boil, then lower the heat and simmer, covered, for 45 minutes.
4. When the liquid is reduced and the lamb is tender, remove the meat and slice it thinly. Place on heated serving platter with the sauce poured over, and sprinkle with chopped parsley.

Serves 4-6

Rosemary/Ramerino

Since the Middle Ages, this sweet-smelling herb has been associated with the Virgin Mary. In a wedding, the bride would always be followed by someone carrying a bouquet of rosemary, and it is one of the four herbs — parsley, sage, rosemary and thyme — known for magical curative powers. In Italian cooking, it is used liberally in *abbachio in padella*, and in other young lamb and suckling pig recipes.

Agnello in Salsa d'Uovo

Lamb in Egg Sauce

This is a very popular way to cook lamb. The meat is stewed until tender then served with a sauce of lemon and egg yolks. There's a recipe very similar to this one in Greek cooking, but which country invented it first no one knows for sure. It's so good, though, that no one really cares!

Ingredients	Regular	Metric
Lamb, leg or shoulder	2 lbs.	1 kg
Flour	4 oz.	125 ml
Salt	1/2 tsp.	2 ml
Pepper	Pinch	Pinch
Bacon or pork fat, diced	4 oz.	125 ml
Onion, chopped	1/2	1/2
Garlic clove, chopped	1	1
White wine	1 cup	250 ml
Bay leaf, crumbled	1	1
Sage	1/2 tsp.	2 ml
Egg yolks	3	3
Juice of 2 lemons		
Parsley, chopped	1 tbsp.	15 ml

1. Cut the lamb into bite-sized pieces and dredge in flour seasoned with salt and pepper.
2. Cook bacon in a large frying pan until the fat is rendered, then add lamb and cook until browned on all sides. Remove from pot.
3. Add onion and garlic, cook for 5 minutes, then add wine, bay leaf and sage and bring to a boil.
4. Return the lamb to the pot and lower the heat. Simmer, covered, for 1 hour until lamb is tender.
5. Put egg yolks in a bowl and beat until light yellow, then stir in lemon juice.
6. Remove lamb to a heated platter and bring sauce to a boil for a few minutes. Take off the heat and add a few spoonfuls to the egg mixture.
7. Whisk this mixture into the sauce and continue to whisk until the sauce has thickened. Pour the sauce over the lamb, garnish with parsley and serve.

Serves 4-6

▶ *Never add beaten eggs directly to a hot sauce. Instead, "temper" them by mixing them with a little of the hot liquid, then stirring into the sauce slowly.*

Arrosto d'Agnello

Roast Leg of Lamb

The serving of a roast leg of spring lamb is one of the most enduring Easter events in Italy. Today, thanks to modern freezing methods, lamb is available all year round, and is particularly good when it is steam-roasted.

Ingredients	Regular	Metric
Leg of lamb	5 lbs.	2 1/2 kg
Salt	1/2 tsp.	2 ml
Pepper	Pinch	Pinch
Garlic cloves, peeled	6	6
Bay leaves	6	6
Mint	1 tbsp.	15 ml
Red wine	8 oz.	250 ml
Red wine vinegar	4 oz.	125 ml
Water	8 oz.	250 ml

1. Place lamb in a roasting pan and sprinkle with salt and pepper.
2. Make small slits in the surface of the meat with a sharp knife and insert the cloves of garlic, then push a meat thermometer into the thickest section, being very careful not to let it touch the bone.
3. Roast in a 475°F./240°C oven for 1 hour, then lower the heat to 350°F./180°C, and put the bay leaves, mint, wine, vinegar and water into the pan. Roast for 1 hour more, or until the lamb is done as you prefer it.
4. Remove garlic cloves and let the meat stand for 10 minutes to let the juices settle, then place on a heated platter and carve individual servings.

Serves 6-8

Mint Sauce

3 tbsp. mint leaves, washed and chopped finely
3 tbsp. sugar
8 oz. white wine vinegar
Mix all the ingredients together and let stand for several hours before serving. Makes about 1 cup.

Agnellino allo Spiedo

Lamb Kebab

Tender young lamb, placed on skewers with onion, tomato and bacon, and grilled over hot coals.

Ingredients	Regular	Metric
Leg of lamb	3 lbs.	1 1/2 kg
White wine	2 cups	500 ml
White wine vinegar	4 oz.	125 ml
Rosemary	2 tsp.	10 ml
Sage	1 tsp.	5 ml
Garlic cloves, crushed	3	3
Bay leaves	4	4
Onion, sliced	1	1
Salt	1/2 tsp.	2 ml
Pepper	Pinch	Pinch
Pancetta or bacon	8 oz.	250 g
Sweet onions	2	2
Cherry tomatoes	12	12
Parsley, chopped	2 tbsp.	30 ml
Garlic cloves, chopped	2	2
Olive oil	2 oz.	50 ml

1. Trim all the fat from the lamb and cut into 2"/5 cm cubes.
2. Combine the next 9 ingredients and pour over the lamb cubes, stirring well. Cover and refrigerate overnight.
3. Preheat broiler or prepare barbecue.
4. Cut pancetta and onions into chunky, equally-sized pieces. Mix the parsley, garlic and oil together and set aside.
5. Drain lamb and dry on paper towels. Take skewers and alternate cubes with pancetta, onion and tomato, then brush with oil.
6. Place on the barbecue or 6"/15 cm under the broiler, and cook for 8-10 minutes, turning often and basting with oil.
7. A few minutes before serving, brush with parsley-garlic mixture and season with salt and pepper. Serve with noodles or rice.

Serves 6-8

Kebabs

Kebabs are a Turkish specialty, but they are also well-known in Greece and other surrounding countries. Recently, because of the popularity of outdoor barbecues, kebabs have become a summer staple in North America as well.

Although lamb is the meat used most often, liver, fish and chicken can be used instead, and the meat can alternate with green peppers, and whole mushrooms, as well as tomato, onion, and bacon. Authentic and decorative kebab skewers can be purchased at specialty shops to add the extra touch.

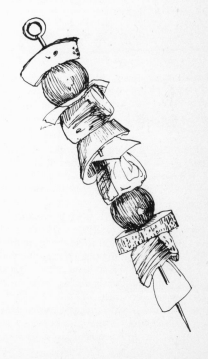

Mint/Menta

Mint is an ancient herb which is mentioned in the Bible as being one of the bitter herbs eaten with the Pascal lamb, and today, the custom of serving mint with lamb is still carried on.

The most common variety is spearmint. It's a perennial and easily grown in the garden, but be sure to enclose the mint bed with stones so that the plant doesn't spread all over the place. Fresh leaves can be used in mint tea, or with vegetables. Small new potatoes are very tasty when they are buttered and shaken with chopped mint, as are carrots, zucchini and sweet young peas. Lamb is always delicious cooked with mint, or served with mint jelly or sauce.

Spezzatino di Agnello

Lamb Stew

In this recipe, you can use less expensive cuts of lamb such as the shoulder, because the slow cooking will make the meat very tender.

Ingredients	Regular	Metric
Oil	4 tbsp.	60 ml
Bacon slices, chopped	4	4
Lamb, cut in cubes	2 lbs.	1 kg
Carrot, sliced	1	1
Onion, chopped	1	1
Tomato, peeled and chopped	1	1
Salt	1/2 tsp.	2 ml
Pepper	Pinch	Pinch
Basil	1/4 tsp.	1 ml
Mint	Pinch	Pinch
Parsley, chopped	2 tbsp.	30 ml
Beef stock	1 cup	250 ml
Tomato paste	1 tbsp.	15 ml
White wine	4 oz.	125 ml

1. Heat the oil in a large pot and cook bacon pieces for 3 minutes, then add the lamb and cook until the cubes are browned on all sides.
2. Add the carrot, onion and tomato, and cook and stir for 5 minutes.
3. Add remaining ingredients, bring to a boil, then lower the heat and simmer for 1 hour or until the lamb is tender. Put extra liquid in if necessary to ensure sufficient sauce.

Serves 4-6

Costolette di Agnello con Peperoni Dolci

Lamb Chops with Sweet Red Peppers

Tender lamb chops sautéed, then served with a piquant sauce of sweet peppers and anchovies.

Ingredients	Regular	Metric
Lamb chops	8	8
Sweet red peppers	2	2
Olive oil	2 oz.	60 ml
Garlic clove, minced	1	1
Anchovy fillets, mashed	3	3
White wine	2 oz.	60 ml
Pepper	Pinch	

1. Heat half the oil in a large frying pan and sauté the garlic for a few seconds. Add the lamb and fry on both sides until cooked. Remove to a serving platter and keep warm.
2. Clean and slice the peppers. Add more oil to the pan and then the peppers. Sauté over medium heat until soft, then add the anchovy fillets. Cook for several minutes more.
3. Add the wine to the pan and deglaze. Cook and stir the sauce until slightly reduced. Season with the pepper.
4. Pour the sauce over the lamb chops and serve immediately.

Serves 4

Lamb Marinade

Some cuts of lamb, like the shank and flank, are better if you marinate them overnight for extra tenderness and flavor. Put one pound of meat in a bowl, and cover with:

  6 oz. red wine
  4 oz. red wine vinegar
  3 oz. olive oil
  Juice of 1 lemon
  2 bay leaves
  3 peeled garlic cloves
  Pinch of mint
  Pinch oregano
  Pinch tarragon
  1/4 tsp. salt
  10 grinds fresh pepper

Add water if necessary until the meat is covered, then leave in the refrigerator for at least 12 hours. Cook according to the recipe, or braise the meat and cook it slowly in the marinade itself.

EGGS
Uova

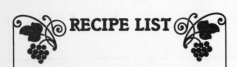
Eggs are strange and wonderful things. Sometimes they need to be beaten before they'll go to work, and sometimes they have to be treated very gently for the best results. They taste wonderful on their own, but also help other ingredients as well. They can be used to bind a sauce, ice a cake or make an omelette, and are one of the most economical sources of protein you can buy.

The egg is nature's perfect food, all done up in its own shell. However you decide to cook eggs, the one basic rule is — don't use too much heat, because they simply don't like it, and will go all tough and sulky if you do. Otherwise, they're marvelous, and can be eaten at any meal in an almost infinite variety of ways. I have given you a few of the ways here, but try inventing your own! The eggs won't mind.

Uova alla Fiorentina

Poached Eggs and Spinach

Poached eggs on buttered bread, ham slices, and a bed of spinach—covered with a creamy sauce and lightly browned grated cheese.

Ingredients	Regular	Metric
Butter, melted	4 tbsp.	60 ml
Bread slices	4	4
Ham or prosciutto slices	8	8
Spinach, cooked and drained	2 cups	500 g
Eggs, poached	8	8
Bechamel sauce	2 cups	500 ml
Mozzarella cheese, grated	1 cup	250 ml
Parmesan cheese, grated	4 oz.	125 ml

1. Pour the butter into a baking dish and preheat the oven to 400°F./ 200°C.
2. Place the bread, trimmed of crusts, in the bottom of the dish. Fold the ham slices over and place 2 on each slice of bread, then cover with spinach.
3. Poach the eggs in boiling water and 4 tablespoons of vinegar for 3 minutes.
4. Put 2 eggs on top of each piece of bread and pour the bechamel sauce over the top, then sprinkle with grated mozzarella and parmesan.
5. Cook in the oven for 5-10 minutes, or until the cheese browns lightly on top. Then carefully lift out 1 bread slice per person, and transfer to individual plates. Serve immediately.

Serves 4

▶ *Poach eggs in advance and store them in a bowl of water in the refrigerator. They will keep for up to two days, and can be warmed whenever they are needed by lowering them into lightly simmering water for two minutes. This is very useful for individual servings – people can dip the eggs into the water themselves and have an almost instant breakfast – or for making dishes like Eggs Benedict or Uova all Fiorentina.*

Frittata

The frittata is an Italian omelette which differs from the French variety in two ways. Ingredients are added to the egg mixture before it is cooked, and it is cooked on both sides and served cut in wedges like a pie, instead of being folded over.

The easiest way to cook it is this. Heat 2 oz. of olive oil in a large frying pan until it is hot but not smoking. Add the egg mixture with whatever ingredients you want to include, then turn the heat down. Pull the eggs away from the sides of the pan, and tip it so the uncooked eggs run underneath and begin to cook. You can also make holes in the bottom of the frittata as it cooks to let the oil and uncooked eggs meld together. When the frittata is slightly brown on the bottom, slip the firm mixture onto a large plate, then invert the frying pan over the plate and turn the whole thing over so the frittata ends up in the pan again, cooking on the other side for several minutes until really firm.

Another method is to place the browned omelette in a preheated 350°F. oven for 10 minutes, or under the broiler until the top is firm and golden.

Frittata con Legume

Vegetable Frittata

Mushrooms, zucchini, asparagus and tomato are the colorful vegetables in this frittata, although almost any kind of vegetables can be used—even left-overs.

Ingredients	Regular	Metric
Olive oil	3 tbsp.	45 ml
Onion, chopped	1/2	1/2
Mushrooms, sliced	8	8
Zucchini, sliced thinly	1	1
Asparagus, peeled and chopped	4	4
Tomato, chopped	1	1
Salt	1 tsp.	5 ml
Pepper	1/4 tsp.	1 ml
Eggs	8-10	8-10
Flour	4 tbsp.	60 ml
Milk	4 tbsp.	60 ml

1. Heat the oil in a large frying pan and cook the onion for 5 minutes, then add the mushrooms, zucchini and asparagus and cook another 5 minutes.
2. Add tomato and half the seasonings and cook for 2 minutes.
3. Beat the eggs with the remaining salt and pepper. Mix the flour and milk together and whisk into the eggs. Pour mixture into the pan, and when the bottom begins to cook, lift the edges to let the liquid run down the side and cook too.
4. When no more liquid remains and the bottom is lightly browned, hold a plate firmly over the top of the pan with one hand, and turn the pan upside down with the other so that the frittata lands on the plate. Then slip it back in the skillet, cooked side up, and brown on the other side briefly. Cut in wedges and serve.

Serves 4

Frittata con Salsiccie

Frittata with Sausage

This delicious omelette contains different ingredients which go together beautifully—cheeses, sausage, onions and tomatoes.

Ingredients	Regular	Metric
Olive oil	2 oz.	50 ml
Eggs	12	12
Flour	4 tbsp.	60 ml
Cream or milk	4 oz.	125 ml
Mozzarella cheese, grated	4 oz.	125 ml
Parmesan cheese, grated	4 oz.	125 ml
Sausage, cooked and thinly sliced	12 oz.	375 g
Salt	1/2 tsp.	2 ml
Pepper	Pinch	Pinch
Green onions, chopped	4	4
Tomatoes, peeled and chopped	2	2

1. Preheat oven to 350°F./180°C.
2. Heat the oil in a large frying pan. Beat the eggs with flour which has been blended with milk, then pour into pan and add all the other ingredients.
3. When the mixture begins to get firm, put it into the oven and cook for 20 minutes.
4. Turn out onto a heated platter, cut into wedges and serve immediately.

Serves 4-6

The traditional way to cook a frittata was to firm it up in a large frying pan, then loosen the edges and toss the omelette up and over like a flapjack so it could cook on the other side. Years ago, when a young Italian girl was finally able to pick up the heavy pan and flip the frittata over without any help whatsoever, custom decreed that she was ready to get married. Nowadays, not so much importance is attached to flipping, and people use methods which are easier than the old-fashioned one.

Uova en Cocotte

Shirred Eggs with Parmesan Cheese

Eggs cooked in ramekins or "cocotte" dishes, with prosciutto and parmesan cheese. Serve as is, or turn out onto rounds of hot buttered toast.

Ingredients	Regular	Metric
Olive oil	1 tbsp.	15 ml
Eggs	4	4
Salt	1/2 tsp.	2 ml
Prosciutto or ham	2 slices	2 slices
Parmesan cheese, grated	2 tbsp.	30 ml
Butter, melted	2 tbsp.	30 ml

1. Preheat the oven to 350°F./180°C.
2. Grease 4 ramekins or shirred-egg dishes with oil, then break one egg into each of them. Sprinkle with salt.
3. Cut the ham into fine slivers and put over the eggs, then cover with cheese and melted butter.
4. Place the ramekins in a pan of water and cook for 10 minutes in the oven, or until the whites are set and the cheese is lightly browned. Serve immediately.

Serves 4

Shirred Eggs

There are many different and delightful-looking baking dishes or *ramekins* available, but the most important thing to remember is that baked eggs must always be cooked in a water bath.

After putting the ingredients into the ramekins, break the eggs on top, and place the ramekins in a shallow pan with just enough water to come two-thirds of the way up the sides, then cook until the whites are firm and the yolks are just soft.

Don't overcook, as the heat from the ramekins will continue to cook the eggs after they have been taken from the oven.

Uova al Piatto con Acciughe

Shirred Eggs with Anchovy Sauce

Eggs baked with anchovies and mozzarella cheese. Always remember to put the ramekins in a pan of water before baking.

Ingredients	Regular	Metric
Butter	4 tbsp.	60 ml
Pepper	Pinch	Pinch
Eggs	4	4
Anchovy fillets	8	8
Mozzarella cheese, shredded	2 oz.	50 ml

1. Preheat oven to 350°F./180°C.
2. Butter four ramekins or shirred-egg dishes, and sprinkle in a little pepper.
3. Break one egg into each one and cover with 1 anchovy fillet and some cheese.
4. Place in a pan of water and cook in the oven for 10 minutes, or until the whites are set and cheese is lightly browned.
5. Meanwhile, heat the rest of the butter with 4 anchovy fillets, minced. Stir until well-blended.
6. Pour the sauce over the cooked eggs and serve immediately.

Serves 4

► *Baking or shirring eggs is an attractive and unusual way to serve them at any meal – from breakfast to a light lunch or supper. They are ideal for brunch, and can be cooked with diced bacon, pancetta, capocollo, sliced prosciutto, cooked mushrooms, and many different types of vegetables. Asparagus tips are especially good.*

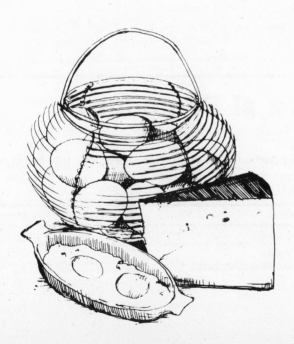

Uova Strapazzate Italia

Scrambled Eggs with Green and Red Peppers

A simple and attractive dish featuring the colors of Italy—green, red and white.

Ingredients	Regular	Metric
Butter	4 tbsp.	60 ml
Red pepper, chopped	1	1
Green pepper, chopped	1	1
Eggs	8	8
Salt	1/2 tsp.	2 ml
Pepper	Pinch	Pinch
Parmesan cheese, grated	4 tbsp.	60 ml

1. Heat the butter in a frying pan and cook the peppers for 3 minutes.
2. Beat the eggs with the salt and pepper and add to the pan. Scramble gently until eggs are almost firm, then add the cheese and stir for 30 seconds more. Serve immediately so the eggs don't overcook.

Serves 4

Uova al Pomodoro

Eggs Poached in Tomato Sauce

Eggs are poached in tomato sauce instead of water in this recipe. The wine and anchovy fillets add a piquant flavor to a dish which can be served at any meal.

Ingredients	Regular	Metric
Tomato sauce	1 cup	250 ml
White wine	4 oz.	125 ml
Anchovy fillets, chopped	4	4
Butter	4 tbsp.	60 ml
Parsley, chopped	1 tbsp.	15 ml
Pepper	Pinch	Pinch
Eggs	8	8

1. Heat the tomato sauce in a frying pan and add the wine, anchovies, butter, parsley and pepper.

➤ *When poaching eggs, never put salt in the cooking water or the whites will separate and become stringy. Use vinegar instead to coagulate the whites and make them firm.*

170

2. When the sauce starts to bubble, break the eggs into the liquid very gently, and arrange them so that they don't touch one another.
3. Cover the pan and simmer for 5 minutes, or until the whites are firm.
4. Remove eggs and place on slices of thin toast, then pour the sauce on top and serve immediately.

Serves 4-6

Omelette con Gamberetti

Shrimp Omelette

If it is too difficult making the large omelette, just make 4 individual omelettes with 2 eggs each. If you do this, however, you must be sure to keep all the omelettes warm until you are ready to serve them.

Ingredients	Regular	Metric
Butter	2 tbsp.	30 ml
Baby shrimps, drained	8 oz. can	250 g can
Eggs	8	8
Salt	1/2 tsp.	2 ml
Pepper	Pinch	Pinch
Olive oil	2 tbsp.	30 ml

1. Heat butter in a small pan and cook shrimps gently for 5 minutes.
2. Beat the eggs with salt and pepper.
3. Heat the oil in a large frying pan and pour the egg mixture in. Draw the mixture away from the sides of the pan so the omelette cooks quickly.
4. When the bottom has started to set, put the shrimps on top and continue to cook until the top is set. Fold over once and serve garnished with parsley sprigs.

Serves 4

➤ *To help keep eggs fresh as long as possible, always store them in the cardboard container they came in on the lowest shelf in the refrigerator. This will keep them at the right temperature, and prevent air penetration which could cause moisture loss.*

171

VEGETABLES

Vegetali

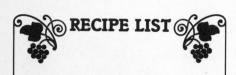
Vegetables are important in Italian meals, and are often served as the main course for a light lunch or supper.

If they are accompanying meat or fish, they are sometimes served in separate small dishes at the side, and the diners can help themselves, but they can also be arranged artistically on the plate before serving for a nice presentation.

Rich in vitamins and minerals, vegetables are a valuable source of fiber, and the green leafy ones are especially high in iron. The most important thing for the cook, however, is that they taste good, and look beautiful with their different shapes and vivid colors. Try not to overcook your vegetables. Some people like them soft, but just remember that these vegetables not only lose their color and taste, but much of their nutrition as well. So cook them until they are tender, but still have a bit of substance, *al dente*, and if you are boiling them, make sure the water is at a full boil before you add them. This way, you will reduce the loss of vitamins and preserve the color.

If you treat your vegetables properly, they will reward you with a feast for both the eyes and the taste-buds.

Melanzane alla Parmigiana

Eggplant Casserole with Parmesan Cheese

This is a wonderful main course dish when you want something meatless. One of Parma's most famous dishes.

Ingredients	Regular	Metric
Eggplants	2	2
Flour	4 tbsp.	60 ml
Salt	1/2 tsp.	2 ml
Pepper	Pinch	Pinch
Oregano	Pinch	Pinch
Eggs, beaten	4	4
Olive oil	4 oz.	125 ml
Tomato sauce	2 cups	500 ml
Mozzarella cheese, grated	1 cup	250 ml
Parmesan cheese, grated	4 oz.	125 ml
Bechamel sauce	1 cup	250 ml

1. Peel eggplants and slice into $1/2$"/1 cm slices, then dredge in flour mixed with salt, pepper and oregano.
2. Dip slices in beaten egg until well-coated.
3. Heat oil in a large frying pan and cook eggplant for 1 minute on each side, adding more oil if necessary.
5. Pour a little tomato sauce in the bottom of a casserole dish, and cover with a layer of eggplant slices.
6. Mix half the mozzarella cheese with the rest of the tomato sauce, parmesan cheese, and bechamel sauce. Pour a little of this mixture over eggplant slices, and continue to layer, ending with sauce.
7. Cover with remaining mozzarella cheese, and bake in a preheated 350°F./180°C oven for 40 minutes. Turn off heat and let sit in oven 5 minutes more. Remove and serve.

Serves 4-6

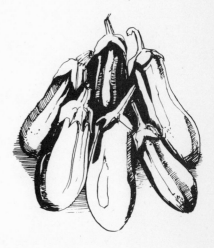

Eggplant/Melanzane

Eggplant is a beautiful-looking vegetable which has been cultivated in Italy since the 15th century, and is extremely popular in the entire Mediterranean region.

It should be firm to the touch and a long way from full maturity. Look for young small ones with smooth shiny skin, and no sign of wrinkling or blemishes. Try to use it right away, but if you can't, keep it in the crisper compartment of the refrigerator for several days.

Cut off the cap and stem when ready to use, and if you've had the bad luck to get an older plant, peel the skin off as it will be bitter. Younger skin is very tasty, however, and may be left on. If slicing, sprinkle the meat with lemon juice as it discolors very quickly. The classic method of cooking involves coating and frying in oil, but eggplant can also be baked, broiled or stewed.

Caponata

Green Peppers and Eggplant

A tasty combination of vegetables—onions, green peppers, eggplant, mushrooms and tomatoes—flavored lightly with chili peppers.

Ingredients	Regular	Metric
Olive oil	4 tbsp.	60 ml
Onions, sliced thinly	2	2
Green peppers, sliced	4	4
Eggplant, peeled and diced	1	1
Mushrooms, quartered	4	4
Tomatoes, peeled and chopped	2	2
Chili peppers	1/4 tsp.	1 ml
Basil	1/4 tsp.	1 ml
Salt	1/2 tsp.	2 ml
Pepper	Pinch	Pinch

1. Heat oil in a large frying pan and cook the onions, green peppers, eggplant and mushrooms for 5 minutes, stirring occasionally.
2. Lower the heat, add the tomatoes and seasonings and simmer for 10 minutes. Serve with chicken, game or pork.

Serves 4-6

Asparagi con Formaggio

Asparagus Baked with Cheese

Substitute tender young white asparagus if you're lucky enough to find it.

Ingredients	Regular	Metric
Asparagus	2 lbs.	1 kg
White wine	4 oz.	125 ml
Butter	8 tbsp.	120 ml
Parmesan cheese, grated	4 oz.	125 ml
Mozzarella cheese, grated	2 oz.	50 ml
Salt	1/2 tsp.	2 ml
Pepper	Pinch	Pinch

▶ *Never drink red wine with asparagus. The slightly sulphurous qualities of the vegetable will give the wine a metallic taste.*

▶ *Don't waste anything when cooking asparagus. Peel the broken-off ends, and place them in the cooking water with the asparagus spears. Then, when the tender shoots are removed to be eaten, chop the ends and put back in the water. Bring to a boil, then take off the heat and stir in a little heavy cream, season with salt, pepper and a dash of paprika, and eat as a wonderful soup.*

1. Wash asparagus thoroughly under running water and peel tough ends.
2. Place in a baking dish and pour white wine over the top, then sprinkle with the cheeses, salt and pepper, and bake in a preheated 375°F./190°C oven for 15 minutes.
3. Lift the asparagus out very carefully and place on a heated platter.
4. Pour the liquid on top and serve immediately.

Serves 4-6

Asparagus/Asparagi

Asparagus is a delicious and refined vegetable which is considered to be a great delicacy. It is usually green, but white varieties are produced in parts of Europe by keeping the sun away from the shoots while they are growing. So prized are these fresh, tender spears that when they are harvested, many towns hold week-long asparagus festivals. White asparagus is difficult to find in North America, however, so most people still eat the green kind.

Look for stalks of equal size, which are straight, crisp and thick. Generally, the thicker the stalk, the more tender it will be when cooked — as long as the bud cluster is tightly closed, and the stalks are a deep healthy green. Otherwise, a thick stalk might be woody.

Wash very carefully to remove all sand and grit by swishing gently in a sinkful of warm water with a little salt added, and rinsing under cold running water until clean. Break off stems where they snap easily, then even the ends up with a sharp knife.

With a vegetable scraper, lightly peel the stalks from just under the tips right to the ends, then lay the asparagus in a large frying pan. Cover with water and a pinch of salt — bring to a boil, and then lower the heat and simmer, uncovered, for 8-12 minutes. Keep your eyes on them, though, because the minute they turn a bright, vivid green, they are done, and should be removed immediately with a slotted spoon and drained on paper towels.

Serve at once, drizzled with melted butter or lemon, and if you worry about etiquette, remember that it is perfectly correct to pick up the spears one at a time and eat them with your fingers.

Pomodori Ripieni al Forno

Baked Stuffed Tomatoes

Delicious served with salad and bread for a complete lunch, or as a vegetable with meat or fish dishes.

Ingredients	Regular	Metric
Tomatoes	6	6
Parmesan cheese, grated	4 oz.	125 ml
Olive oil	4 oz.	125 ml
Garlic cloves, minced	2	2
Ground veal	4 oz.	125 g
Oregano	Pinch	Pinch
Salt	1/2 tsp.	2 ml
Pepper	Pinch	Pinch
Egg	1	1
Parsley, chopped	2 tbsp.	30 ml
Sugar	1 tbsp.	15 ml
Breadcrumbs	4 oz.	125 ml

1. Wash tomatoes and slice a little bit off the tops and bottoms so they will sit straight, then cut in half crossways and place in oiled baking sheet.
2. Scoop a little tomato pulp out of each half for the stuffing.
3. Put pulp in a bowl along with the other ingredients and mix well.
4. Divide into 12 equal portions and press 1 portion into each tomato half, then cook in a preheated 350°F./180°C oven for 40 minutes and serve hot.

Serves 4-6

Parsley/Prezzemolo

I always keep parsley on hand in my kitchen. It is not only is good in cooking, but also adds color to the plate for presentation. Try using Italian parsley, the one with the broad leaves. It is more pungent than other varieties. When using in frying always add at the end of the recipe, or the heat will turn the parsley black.

Cipollini al Forno

Baked Onions

Onions baked in the oven to preserve their sweetness, then topped with a piquant mustard dressing. The perfect accompaniment to lamb or pork dishes.

Ingredients	Regular	Metric
Small pearl onions	1 1/2 lbs.	750 g
Oil	4 oz.	125 ml
Dry mustard	1 tsp.	5 ml
White vinegar	2 tbsp.	30 ml
Salt	1/2 tsp.	2 ml
Pepper	Pinch	Pinch
Sage	Pinch	Pinch
Red pepper, sliced	1	1

1. Peel the onions and blanch in boiling water for a few minutes, then drain well and toss with a little oil.
2. Place in a baking dish and cook in a preheated 350°F./180°C oven for 20 minutes.
3. Mix the oil, mustard, vinegar, salt and pepper, and sage in a bowl and pour over the onions. Decorate with thinly sliced red pepper, and serve hot or cold.

Serves 4-6

Onion/Cipolle

The onion is essential to Italian cooking in many forms.

Miniature whites. Pickle for use in plates of antipasto, or use unpickled in stews, or creamed with green peas.

Cooking onions. Excellent for cooking in sauces and stews, especially the yellow-skinned variety which is 2 or 3 inches wide, because they don't become too sweet or mushy.

Sweet onions. Bermuda, Spanish, and Italian are mild enough to eat raw. The Italian onion is shaped like a large egg, and can be yellow, white or red. Although these mild onions don't cause as many tears when they are chopped, they aren't quite as good for cooking.

Whatever kind you buy, make sure the onions are firm and well-shaped with the papery skins dry and shiny. Reject onions with soft spots, stains, green spots, or sprouts growing out of the necks.

Store in a cool dry place with good air circulation, and they should last for a month or two.

▶ *Don't refrigerate onions, as this will cause dampness, sprouting, and decay. If you want to keep part of an onion which has already been cut, however, you can wrap it tightly in foil or plastic wrap and refrigerate — as long as you use it within a couple of days.*

Piselli in Padella

Peas and Onions

If you can get peas that are very tender, you won't have to boil them in water first, just sauté them along with the onions and prosciutto.

Ingredients	Regular	Metric
Peas	1 lb.	500 g
Oil	4 tbsp.	60 ml
Onion, chopped	1	1
Garlic clove, chopped	1	1
Ham or prosciutto, chopped	2 oz.	50 ml
Oregano	Pinch	Pinch
Basil	Pinch	Pinch
Salt	1/2 tsp.	2 ml
Pepper	Pinch	Pinch

1. Shell the peas and wash. Cook in boiling water for 5 minutes, then drain.
2. Heat the oil in a large frying pan and cook the onion and garlic for 5 minutes.
3. Add the prosciutto, peas and seasonings, and cook 3-5 minutes more. Serve immediately.

Serves 4

Patate alla Casalinga

Home Fried Potatoes

Potatoes cooked this way are never as good as when they are made at home, so they are called home-style—"alla casalinga". Delicious served at breakfast with eggs and sausage.

Ingredients	Regular	Metric
Potatoes	6	6
Oil	4 tbsp.	60 ml
Butter	2 tbsp.	30 ml
Salt	1/2 tsp.	2 ml
Pepper	Pinch	Pinch

➤ *White vegetables, such as potatoes and cauliflower, can be kept from discoloring by adding a pinch of cream of tartar to the cooking water. Rice will stay white with the addition of a little lemon juice.*

	Regular	Metric
Green pepper, chopped	1	1
Paprika	1 tsp.	5 ml
Parsley, chopped	1 tbsp.	15 ml

1. Cook potatoes for 20-30 minutes until just soft, then cool and slice.
2. Heat the oil and butter in a large frying pan, and add salt and pepper.
3. Add potato slices and cook until golden brown on both sides, then add peppers and paprika and cook for another 5 minutes. Sprinkle with parsley just before serving.

Serves 4-6

Patate Ripiene al Formaggio

Stuffed Baked Potatoes

The kind of cheese you use in this recipe is up to you. I prefer sharp cheddar, but if you want a stringy consistency, mozzarella is good.

Ingredients	Regular	Metric
Baking potatoes, large	4	4
Butter	4 tbsp.	60 ml
Green onions, chopped	4	4
Ham, chopped	4 oz.	125 ml
Cheese, grated	4 tbsp.	60 ml
Parsley, chopped	2 tbsp.	30 ml
Sour cream	4 oz.	125 ml
Salt	1/2 tsp.	2 ml
Pepper	Pinch	Pinch

1. Bake the potatoes in the oven until soft, then cut in half.
2. Heat the butter in a frying pan and cook the onion, green onions and ham for 5 minutes.
3. Scoop the potato out of the shells and add to the pan with all the other ingredients. Mash until potato is smooth and ingredients are mixed into it well.
4. Put mixture back in the potato shells and put back in the oven. When tops are golden brown, remove and serve.

Serves 4-6

Potato/Patate

The Spanish brought the potato back from Ecuador in 1553, calling it by its native name *battato*. By 1558, it was well-established as a vegetable in Italy, although it didn't become popular in other European countries until much later. The best potatoes for baking are russets or Idahoes because of their mealy texture.

Never bake a potato in foil as moisture will be held in, and the potato will end up being steamed instead of baked. Instead, wash and dry the potato and place in a preheated 425°F. oven. If you want a shiny skin, rub it first with butter or olive oil. After twenty minutes, turn the potato over, and prick the skin with a fork to let out the moisture. Then continue to cook for another 25 to 35 minutes.

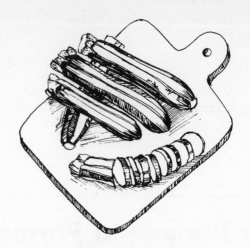

Zucchini

Zucchini in Italian means baby marrow, and that's exactly what you should buy. Always get the small or medium-sized zucchini, or if you grow your own, pick them young. Large zucchini look spectacular but are not nearly as tender and tasty as the little ones.

Zucchini Impannati

Breaded Zucchini

Long quarters of tender zucchini, coated in breadcrumbs and sautéed until golden brown.

Ingredients	Regular	Metric
Oil	1 cup	250 ml
Zucchini	6	6
Flour	4 oz.	125 ml
Eggs, beaten	2	2
Milk	4 oz.	125 ml
Breadcrumbs	1 cup	250 ml
Oregano	1/2 tsp.	2 ml
Sugar	1 tbsp.	15 ml
Salt	1/2 tsp.	2 ml
Pepper	Pinch	Pinch

1. Heat oil in a large frying pan.
2. Wash zucchini and cut in quarters, lengthwise.
3. Dredge in flour, then dip in eggs and milk beaten together. Mix the breadcrumbs with the sugar and the seasonings, and press the zucchini into the mixture until well-coated.
4. Cook in hot oil until golden brown all over, then drain on paper towels and serve.

Serves 4-6

180

Zucchini del Contadini

Zucchini Farmers' Style

Zucchini boats, stuffed with mushrooms and cheese and baked until crisp and bubbly on top. Medium-sized zucchini are the best for this recipe.

Ingredients	Regular	Metric
Zucchini	4	4
Breadcrumbs	4 oz.	125 ml
Olive oil	4 tbsp.	60 ml
Eggs, beaten	2	2
Parmesan cheese, grated	4 oz.	125 ml
Mushrooms, chopped	8	8
Pepper	Pinch	Pinch
Oregano	Pinch	Pinch

1. Place zucchini in pan and cover with water, then bring to a boil and cook for 4 minutes.
2. Remove and slice in half lengthwise. Scoop out the pulp and put in a bowl, reserving the shells.
3. Add remaining ingredients to the pulp and mix thoroughly. Fill the zucchini shells with this mixture, and sprinkle with more parmesan cheese.
4. Place on oiled baking sheet and cook in a preheated 350°F./180°C oven for 20 minutes. Remove and serve immediately.

Serves 4

➤ *To prevent spoiling a recipe, always break an egg into a saucer before adding it to other ingredients, just in case it's not as good as it should be.*

➤ *To save time at dinner, cook your vegetables well in advance until they are just crisply tender, then plunge them immediately into cold water to stop them cooking and to preserve their color. Just before serving, heat them quickly in a little butter, or put briefly into boiling water. This method, called "refreshing", is used by professional chefs in the best restaurants, but can be used just as successfully at home.*

Artichoke/Carciofi

The artichoke is a beautiful vegetable which you can cook whole or fill with a delicious stuffing. The artichoke heart is the most delectable part.

An artichoke heart consists of the bottom, the fuzzy choke (which is edible in very young artichokes), and the soft inner leaves — what remains after the outer leaves and stems have been removed. Since tender, young artichokes are hard to find, most of us use canned hearts packed in oil. Drain them well before using in salads or recipes.

Look for artichokes with the leaves hugging each other closely — once the leaves have started to open, the artichoke is over the hill. The leaves should also be plump, fresh-looking, and bright-green.

Wash before cooking by swishing the artichokes around in warm water with a little salt added, then rinsing under cold, running water. Have ready a bowl of lemon juice and water, to use so that the cut parts of the vegetable don't turn brown.

To prepare for cooking, lay the artichoke on its side and cut off the top third of the head with a sharp knife, then snip the points off the leaves with a pair of scissors. Remove and discard any tough-looking leaves at the bottom by the stem. Rub any cut parts immediately with lemon juice, and set the vegetables in a lemon bath until ready to cook.

To steam and eat whole, cut off the bottoms of the stems, stand the artichokes up in a pan, and add 1 inch of salted water along with a couple of spoonfuls of lemon juice.

Carciofi Ripieni Napolitana

Stuffed Artichokes Neapolitan Style

Eat your way into this delicious vegetable leaf by leaf, then savor the tender heart. What a beautiful dish!

Ingredients	Regular	Metric
Artichokes	4	4
Juice of 1 lemon		
Eggs	2	2
Salt	1/2 tsp.	2 ml
Pepper	Pinch	Pinch
Parmesan cheese, grated	4 oz.	125 ml
Anchovies, minced	2	2
Parsley, chopped	1 tbsp.	15 ml
Breadcrumbs	4 oz.	125 ml
Olive oil	4 tbsp.	60 ml
White wine	4 oz.	125 ml

1. Cut 1"/2 cm off the tops of the artichokes, and the spiky ends off the other leaves. Remove tough bottom leaves and cut the stems so the artichokes can stand upright, then rub all the cut areas with lemon juice to prevent discoloration.
2. Remove the chokes by spreading the leaves and scooping out the furry part with a spoon.
3. Beat the eggs in a bowl, then add the salt, pepper, cheese, anchovies, parsley and breadcrumbs. Mix well and then stuff into the center and around the leaves of the artichokes.
4. Stand the artichokes up in a baking dish and sprinkle with the oil and wine. Cover the dish and place in a preheated 375°F./190°C oven for 30 minutes. Uncover and cook the artichokes for 10-15 minutes more until the leaves come off easily. Serve immediately.

Serves 4

Fagiolini Stufati

Green Beans and Tomatoes

This is a dish which is very popular in all the Mediterranean countries, and which actually tastes better the next day—hot or cold.

Ingredients	Regular	Metric
Green beans	2 lbs.	1 kg
Olive oil	4 tbsp.	60 ml
Onion, sliced	1	1
Garlic cloves, minced	2	2
Tomatoes, peeled and chopped	6	6
Basil	1/2 tsp.	2 ml
Oregano	Pinch	Pinch
Thyme	Pinch	Pinch
Salt	1/2 tsp.	2 ml
Pepper	Pinch	Pinch

1. Prepare the beans and cook in boiling salted water for 5 minutes, then remove and drain.
2. Meanwhile, heat the oil in a large frying pan and cook the onion and garlic for 5 minutes.
3. Add the tomatoes and seasonings and simmer for 10 minutes. Add the drained beans and cook for 5 minutes more. Serve immediately or put in the refrigerator and serve chilled.

Serves 4-6

Cover the pan, and steam for 20 to 40 minutes — depending on the size of the artichokes. They are done when the leaves pull off easily. Remove carefully (they'll be hot) and drain upside down on paper towels, then eat right away or serve chilled.

Eating an artichoke is, for some of us, a rapturous experience. The more you eat it, the better it gets. Serve with a dipping bowl of vinaigrette, melted butter, or mayonnaise mixed with lemon juice. Then pull off the leaves, one at a time, dip the soft part into the sauce, and scrape this delicate flesh off by pulling the end of the leaf between your teeth. Discard the rest of the leaf in a bowl.

When you get to the pale little leaves in the center, cut them away from the bottom, along with the choke, being very careful not to take away any of the bottom meat. Now take a knife and fork, and eat this beautiful-tasting prize very slowly, savoring every bite.

Green Beans/Fagiolini

Green beans used to be called "string beans" because of the tough strings which had to be removed from the sides of the pods, but fortunately modern day botany has eliminated this tiresome chore. To keep the beans a vivid green color, they should be cooked very quickly in a large amount of rapidly boiling water. Snip off the ends, and for more flavor, leave them whole, then add a few at a time to the water so that it will remain at a high boil.

Professional chefs sometimes heat a large knife over the flame, then plunge it into the pot along with the beans to keep the water boiling as briskly as possible. Start tasting the beans after five minutes, and remove them as soon as they are tender but crisp.

Fennel/Finocchio

Florentine fennel is a native of Italy, and is called finocchio or cartucci. It is usually prepared the same way as a root of celery, and its pleasant, slightly liquorice taste makes it particularly good with fish.

Finocchio al Forno

Baked Fennel

Florentine fennel, commonly called finocchio, has stalks like celery, and the licorice flavor of anise. If you have never tried it, this dish will provide a tasty introduction.

Ingredients	Regular	Metric
Fennel, bunches	4	4
Salt	1/2 tsp.	2 ml
Pepper	Pinch	Pinch
Butter	2 oz.	50 ml
Parmesan cheese, grated	4 oz.	125 ml

1. Chop off the tops and the hard bottoms of the fennel and wash thoroughly under running water, then cut in quarters.
2. Put in a large pot and cover with water. Bring to a boil and cook for 10-15 minutes until tender, then remove and drain.
3. Heat oven to 350°F./120°C and place fennels in a buttered baking dish. Season with salt and pepper, top with butter, and sprinkle with cheese.
5. Cook in the oven for 15 minutes or until cheese is melted, then serve immediately.

Serves 4-6

Spinaci al Formaggio

Spinach with Cheese

This is a wonderful way to cook spinach. The onion and grated cheese enhance the flavor of the greens, and the simple method of cooking preserves their freshness.

Ingredients	Regular	Metric
Spinach	2 lbs.	1 kg
Oil	2 tbsp.	30 ml
Butter	2 tbsp.	30 ml

Onion, chopped	1	1
Parmesan cheese, grated	4 tbsp.	60 ml
Salt	1/2 tsp.	2 ml
Pepper	Pinch	Pinch

1. Wash spinach thoroughly and remove any tough stems. Let drain and pour off excess moisture.
2. Heat the oil and butter in a large pot and cook onions for 5 minutes.
3. Add the spinach and cover. Cook for 3-5 minutes, or until spinach is tender and moisture has evaporated.
4. Stir in cheese, salt and pepper, and serve immediately.

Serves 4-6

▶ *Freeze chopped onion in ice cube trays, and then use when needed — just throw the square right in the pan and cook as usual.*

Spinach/Spinaci

Spinach must be washed carefully before cooking to get out all the gritty sand. Swirl the leaves vigorously in a sinkful of warm water with a little salt added. Then repeat rinsings in cold water until thoroughly clean. Remove tough stems and cook the spinach for 3-5 minutes in a covered pot with just the water clinging to the leaves. Put in a strainer and press out any excess moisture, then leave whole or chop.

Peppers/Peperoni

Sweet peppers – **peperoni dolci** – are versatile and tasty. The bell pepper is red and sweet when ripened to maturity, but is green when picked before it has ripened all the way. Italian sweet peppers are longer and narrower, and have a slightly stronger taste.

Look for glossy firm peppers with no shrivelled skin or injuries, and a well-developed shape. Keep in plastic or foil in the refrigerator for several days.

Sauté quickly in oil for sauces, use on top of pizza, or stuff with rice and meat. If baking stuffed, rub shell with oil before putting in the oven.

Peperoni Ripieni al Pomodoro

Stuffed Green Peppers with Tomato Sauce

This recipe, which combines vegetables, meat, rice, eggs, cheese and oil, is a well-balanced meal just by itself. It is also very filling, and can easily be used as a main course dish.

Ingredients	Regular	Metric
Large green peppers	4	4
Ground veal	1 lb.	500 g
Breadcrumbs	4 oz.	125 ml
Cooked rice	1 cup	250 ml
Bacon slices, chopped	4	4
Salt	1/2 tsp.	2 ml
Pepper	Pinch	Pinch
Basil	Pinch	Pinch
Eggs	3	3
Parmesan cheese, grated	4 oz.	125 ml
Olive oil	4 oz.	125 ml
Tomato sauce	1 cup	250 ml

1. Remove stems from the peppers and cut off the tops, then scoop out the seeds and stand the peppers in a baking dish.
2. Mix together all the other ingredients except the tomato sauce, and fill the peppers with equal amounts of this stuffing.
3. Place tops back on and cook in a preheated 375°F./190°C oven for 1 hour.
4. Heat tomato sauce. Place peppers on a serving platter and pour the hot sauce over the tops. Serve immediately.

Serves 4

Verze Fritti

Fried Savoy Cabbage

This is a simple and tasty dish, especially if you use Savoy cabbage. That's the kind with the curly leaves, and it is usually much more tender and mild then other varieties.

Ingredients	Regular	Metric
Head of cabbage	1	1
Garlic clove, chopped	1	1
White wine	4 oz.	125 ml
Butter	4 tbsp.	60 ml
Oil	2 tbsp.	30 ml
Bacon or pancetta slices, chopped	4	4
Salt	1/2 tsp.	2 ml
Pepper	Pinch	Pinch

1. Wash cabbage and discard the core, then slice coarsely and place in a large pot with the garlic clove and wine. Cover and cook for 5 minutes, or until the leaves are soft.
2. Heat butter and oil in a large frying pan and add remaining ingredients.
3. Cook until the fat has been rendered from the bacon, then add drained cabbage.
4. Cook over medium heat for 10 minutes, then serve immediately.

Serves 4

Cabbage/Capucci

The three most common types of cabbage available are the large compact cabbage with greenish-white leaves, red cabbage, and Savoy cabbage, which has loose leaves and is superior in taste. It has a more delicate and nutty flavor than the common cabbage and requires less cooking.

You should cook any cabbage very quickly until just tender but still crisp — it will taste better and won't leave unpleasant odors.

➤ *Always remove the tops from carrots and beets before storing or they will drain all the goodness and moisture out of your vegetables.*

SALADS
Insalata

There are many different kinds of salads, but the top favorite is still *insalata verde*, the simple green salad tossed with a tangy vinaigrette dressing. My favorite kinds of lettuce are Boston and Romaine, but whatever you use, be sure that the greens are absolutely fresh and crisp and torn into pieces with your hands – never cut. Mixing different kinds of lettuces together in one salad looks nice, and creates an interesting taste and texture.

Salads with other ingredients in them are called *insalata mista*, and here's where the cook can really use some imagination. Lately, salads featuring cooked pasta have become more and more popular, which is good, as they are a tasty source of vitamins and energy.

In Italy, the salad is served after the main course, but really it can go anywhere in the meal – from the first thing you eat, to the introduction to the main course, to the last thing you eat before dessert to cleanse the palate.

If wine is being served with the meal, though, it is probably a good idea to have the salad at the beginning, since vinegar and most salad dressings don't go well with wine.

Insalata Verde

Green Salad

A green salad is only as good as its lettuce, so choose carefully and keep it cold and crisp until ready to use.

Ingredients	Regular	Metric
Romaine	1 head	1 head
Olive oil	4 tbsp.	60 ml
Red vinegar	4 tbsp.	60 ml
Dry mustard	1 tsp.	5 ml
Salt	1/2 tsp.	2 ml
Pepper	Pinch	Pinch
Oregano	Pinch	Pinch
Juice of 1 lemon		
Green pepper, sliced	1	1
Cucumber, peeled and sliced	1	1
Tomatoes, cut in wedges	2	2

1. Wash and dry romaine leaves and put in refrigerator until ready to use.
2. Place oil, vinegar, mustard, salt, pepper and oregano in a bowl, and whisk in lemon juice until mixture is smooth.
3. Toss with the lettuce, green pepper and cucumber. Put tomato wedges on top, drizzle with the last of the dressing, and serve.

Serves 4-6

Vinegar/Aceto

Although the Chinese were using rice wine vinegar over 3000 years ago, vinegar was actually given its name by the French back in Roman times. When the wine of the conquerors went bad, the French called it *vinaigre* or sour wine.

Today the wine is deliberately made sour by fermenting it until it is acidic, producing the vinegar most often used in Italian cooking for marinating, and for use in tangy salad dressings.

You can make your own herbal vinegar by adding ingredients like garlic or tarragon to a tightly closed bottle of good wine vinegar, and leaving the flavors to marry until ready to use.

► *When selecting a head of lettuce, press the stem with your thumbs to see if it is hard. The harder the stem, the fresher the lettuce.*

Olive Oil/Olio d'Oliva

The olive is one of the oldest fruits known to man, and its oil has been prized for over five thousand years. For a time it was so valuable that it became an important article of trade and commerce.

The olive tree doesn't start to bear fruit until it is thirty-five years old, and then only the green unripe olives are used for oil. They are crushed in a press, with each pressing producing a different grade of oil.

Extra Virgin Oil. This comes from the first pressing with nothing added, and is excellent for salads.
Virgin Olive Oil. This comes from the second pressing, again with no additives.
Pure Olive Oil. The pressed pulp is now pressed again with solvents.
Fine Olive Oil. The last pressing of the pulp with water added. Not the best for salads, but is good for cooking or frying.

How to buy. Always try to get the best oil you can. It doesn't pay to scrimp because even a small amount of oil contributes a great deal to the taste of the food. It should be a golden color with a not too pungent odor. Try to smell it before buying.

Since olive oil doesn't respond well to light or extremes in temperature, always buy it in a tin or opaque container – never in a glass bottle.

How to store. Refrigerating olive oil makes it cloudy, and some purists think it also changes the taste, but since good oil can be stored on the shelf for about a year, refrigeration isn't always necessary. Keep it in several small light-proof containers. The less air touches the oil, the less likely it is to become rancid.

Insalata di Primavera
Spring Vegetable Salad

In Italian, "primavera" means spring, and a primavera salad should be made with the first tender vegetables to appear in the spring. Any vegetables can be used as long as they are young and small.

Ingredients	Regular	Metric
Lima beans	1 lb.	500 g
Peas	1 lb.	500 g
Baby artichokes	1 lb.	500 g
Small new potatoes	8 oz.	250 g
Red wine vinegar	1 tbsp.	15 ml
Olive oil	3 tbsp.	45 ml
Salt	1/2 tsp.	2 ml
Pepper	Pinch	Pinch
Mayonnaise	1 cup	250 ml
Dry mustard	1/4 tsp.	1 ml
Tarragon	Pinch	Pinch
Eggs, hard-cooked	2	2
Capers	2 tbsp.	30 ml
Sour gherkin, sliced	1	1

1. Shell beans and peas, and cook in salted boiling water until tender.
2. Slice artichokes and cook briefly in boiling water with a little vinegar.
3. Boil or steam potatoes, then cool, peel and slice them.
4. When all the vegetables are cooled, put them in a bowl and toss gently with vinegar, salt and pepper. Then let stand for an hour or two.
5. Mix mayonnaise with the mustard and tarragon, then mix with salad. Garnish with slices of hard-cooked egg, capers, and slices of sour gherkin.

Serves 4-6

Insalata di Broccoli e Pancetta

Broccoli and Bacon

If you want broccoli which is crunchy and flavorful, never overcook it. As soon as it turns bright green it is done.

Ingredients	Regular	Metric
Broccoli	1 lb.	500 g
Bacon	4 oz.	125 g
Garlic clove, minced	1	1
Salt	1/2 tsp.	2 ml

1. Clean broccoli and cut away the tough stems, then cook in boiling salted water until bright green and tender.
2. Meanwhile, cut the bacon into $1/2$"/1 cm pieces, and fry until crisp. Add garlic at the last minute.
3. Put broccoli in a bowl and add bacon pieces and 3 tablespoons of bacon drippings. Sprinkle with salt and toss, then serve immediately.

Serves 4

Broccoli/Broccola

Broccoli is a native of Italy, and was introduced into France and Great Britain at the beginning of the 18th century, although it didn't become popular in North America until after the first world war. The broccoli most highly prized nowadays is a strain called *Calabrese* which is dark green with a purplish tinge.

Spears should be washed carefully, then steamed or cooked quickly in boiling salted water until they are a vivid green and crisply tender. To make sure the stems cook as quickly as the heads, score them lightly with a sharp knife.

Broccoli can be served in a number of ways — hot with a dredging of melted butter, cold with a sauce vinaigrette, or in soups and salads. Don't wash until ready to use, and store tightly wrapped in the refrigerator for up to three days.

► *When choosing an artichoke, choose one with tight leaves, and then squeeze it between your palms. If it squeaks, it is fresh and perfect.*

Fresh Herb Garden

There is nothing like the taste of fresh herbs to liven up a special dish, but with the harsh winters we experience in most parts of the continent, these aren't always available.

However, it's possible to cultivate a small indoor herb garden as long as you have a window with lots of light. The best herbs to grow are parsley, basil, marjoram, dill and rosemary. Plant them in clay pots, and because herbs like good drainage, you should first place stones at the bottom of the pots, then fill them with 1/3 commercial planting soil, and 2/3 sand.

In the summer, of course, you can have an outdoor garden, and plant the herbs you think you will use the most. Basil, for instance, is wonderful for tomato sauce and pesto, and very easy to grow. The trick is to cut the plants back in the early summer and right through July, without ever letting them get to the blossoming period. Then you can either make sauce with them, or freeze them for later use. In any case, give them a good watering down, then pick them the following morning, and dry them in the sun.

Use your frozen herbs unthawed, in the same quantity as fresh – that is, about twice as much as you would use of dried herbs. Don't try to thaw them out and use them as a garnish, though, as they will probably look limp and unattractive.

You can bring summer herbs from outdoors into your inside garden. Just pot them in late summer and keep them in a partially shaded spot so they can adapt slowly, then, when the air starts to get nippy, bring them in for the winter, and for the best taste in your recipes.

Insalata di Carote

Carrot Salad

This salad of carrots, walnuts and raisins, is excellent with all kinds of fish and shellfish.

Ingredients	Regular	Metric
Carrots	1 lb.	500 g
Raisins	1/2 cup	125 ml
Walnuts, chopped	1/2 cup	125 ml
Salt	1/2 tsp.	2 ml
Pepper	Pinch	Pinch
Olive oil	3 tbsp.	45 ml
Red wine vinegar	1 tbsp.	15 ml

1. Peel carrots and shred into long strips on the large-holed side of the grater.
2. Put in a bowl with raisins and nuts, then add salt, pepper and oil, and toss well.
3. Just before serving, toss the vinegar in.

Serves 4

Insalata di Cetrioli e Cipolle

Cucumber and Onion Salad

Cucumber and onion slices in a tangy vinaigrette dressing with anchovies adding the final touch.

Ingredients	Regular	Metric
Anchovy fillets	4	4
Garlic clove, minced	1	1
Olive oil	4 oz.	125 ml
Red wine vinegar	4 oz.	125 ml
Salt	1/2 tsp.	2 ml
Pepper	Pinch	Pinch
Oregano	Pinch	Pinch
Spanish onion, sliced thinly	1	1
Cucumbers, peeled and sliced	2	2
Green onion, chopped	1	1

1. Place anchovies and garlic in a bowl and mash into a paste, then add the oil, vinegar, salt, pepper and oregano and whisk well.
2. Add onions and cucumbers and toss until coated. Put in the refrigerator for at least 1 hour before serving.

Serves 4

Insalata di Pomodoro, Olive, e Cipolle

Tomato, Olive and Onion Salad

This salad is particularly good with breaded fish fillets and veal dishes.

Ingredients	Regular	Metric
Tomatoes	4	4
Green or black pitted olives	4 oz.	125 ml
Onion, sliced thinly	1	1
Basil	1/4 tsp.	1 ml
Olive oil	4 tbsp.	60 ml
Salt	1/2 tsp.	2 ml

1. Core the tomatoes and cut in small wedges.
2. Add the other ingredients and toss well.
3. Put the salad in the refrigerator, and let marinate for at least 1 hour before serving, then serve cold.

Serves 4

➤ *Use sweet, mild red onions in salads, and to make them even more appealing, soak the slices in very cold water for fifteen minutes before serving.*

Insalata di Tanno e Fagioli

Tuna Fish and Bean Salad

If you want to make this dish in just a few minutes, canned beans can be substituted— they're very good and very quick.

Ingredients	Regular	Metric
White kidney beans	1 cup	250 ml
Onion, sliced	1/2	1/2
Tuna fish	7 oz. can	225 g can
Tomato, peeled and chopped	1	1
Salt	1/2 tsp.	2 ml
Pepper	Pinch	Pinch
Olive oil	2 tbsp.	30 ml
Red wine vinegar	2 tbsp.	30 ml

1. Place beans in a bowl, cover with cold water, and let stand overnight.
2. Drain and rinse the beans, then place in a saucepan, cover with fresh cold water and bring to a boil. Reduce heat and simmer for 60 minutes, stirring occasionally. Drain, cool, and place in a salad bowl.
3. Add onion to the bowl. Drain and flake the tuna, and add to the bowl along with the tomato.
4. Stir in the salt, pepper, oil, and vinegar, and toss gently. Serve at room temperature.

Serves 4

Insalata di Broccoletti

Broccoli Vinaigrette

This broccoli with a tangy sauce is good served either hot or cold.

Ingredients	Regular	Metric
Broccoli, large bunch	1	1
Olive oil	4 oz.	125 ml
Red wine vinegar	4 oz.	125 ml
Basil	1 tsp.	5 ml
Oregano	Pinch	Pinch
Thyme	Pinch	Pinch

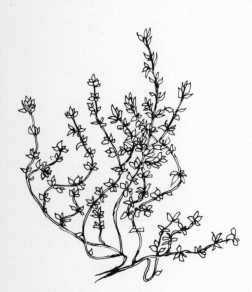

Thyme/Timo

Thyme is excellent for cooking slowly in stews, chowders, or gumbos, and is also good in marinades and with roast beef.

It retains its flavor very well when dried, and is a natural partner of bay. In fact, the bouquet garni is actually composed of these two herbs plus parsley and other alternate ingredients.

Chicken and thyme are a beautiful combination, and with lemon, the taste becomes even better. There is actually a type of thyme with a lemony flavor called lemon thyme, which is more delicate than garden thyme, but if you can't get it, a little lemon added will do just fine.

Tarragon	Pinch	Pinch
Salt	1/2 tsp.	2 ml
Pepper	Pinch	Pinch
Parsley, chopped	1 tbsp.	15 ml

1. Leave broccoli spears whole and cut deeply across the bottoms of the stems.
2. Place upright in a pot and add 2"/5 cm of water, then bring to a boil and cover.
3. Cook for 10 minutes or until broccoli begins to change color. Remove, slice in half lengthwise, and place on heated serving platter.
4. Mix together all remaining ingredients and pour over the broccoli, turning until well-coated. Serve at once or place in the refrigerator for 2 hours and serve chilled.

Serves 4

Vinaigrette Dressing

This is one of the easiest and most useful dressings there is. Use a good light olive oil, and a fine wine vinegar. Taste as you make so that you can adjust the seasonings and have a dressing which is just what you like.

6 oz. olive oil
1 oz. red wine vinegar
Juice of 1 lemon
Pinch of oregano
Freshly ground pepper
Salt
Pinch of garlic powder
1/4 tsp. dried mustard or Dijon

Put all the ingredients together and mix vigorously with a small wire whisk for a smooth consistency.

Makes 1 cup

Mustard/Mostarde

Mustard is very good as a peppy ingredient in sauces and salads, but it's at its best with meats, particularly roast beef and ham.

English mustard is hot, and was first made in Lancastershire around 1730 by a little old lady called Clements. She was the first person to produce a powder which could be turned immediately into a hot paste with just the addition of water, and she kept the secret of her discovery very close to her chest for many years as she rode from town to town and sold her mustard to eager customers – including King George I.

The most famous of French mustards is Dijon, which is made from the ground-up seeds of white mustard grown in the Dijon district. The powder is mixed with white wine producing one of the finest mustards in the world.

Italian Cremona mustard contains finely-chopped chrystallized fruit.

➤ *Bottled mustard loses its freshness very quickly once the jar has been opened, but it helps if you put a thin slice of lemon on top of the mixture before screwing the lid on as tightly as possible. Then all you have to do is replace the lemon slice every week until the mustard is gone.*

Prepared Mustard

To make your own mustard from powder, add about 2 ounces of liquid, water, wine, or even wine vinegar, to 1/4 cup dry mustard, and if it's too hot, add a little olive oil and sugar.

Insalata di Patate Italiana
Italian Style Potato Salad

Potato salad prepared this way is much lighter than potato salad made with mayonnaise.

Ingredients	Regular	Metric
Potatoes, halved	6	6
Olive oil	3 oz.	45 ml
Sweet red peppers, sliced	2	2
Green onions, chopped	1	1
Garlic cloves, chopped	2	2
Red wine vinegar	2 oz.	50 ml
Salt	1/2 tsp.	2 ml
Pepper	Pinch	Pinch
Mustard, mild or Dijon	1/4 tsp.	1 ml
Parsley, chopped	2 tbsp.	30 ml

1. Cook potatoes in boiling salted water for 20 minutes, or until soft but still firm. Remove, hold under cold water for a few minutes to stop cooking, and then let cool.
2. Heat some of the oil in a frying pan, and cook the red pepper, onion and garlic for 5 minutes, then place in a bowl.
3. Peel potatoes and cut into thick french-fry shapes and add to the bowl.
4. Add the rest of the oil, vinegar, salt and pepper, and mustard. Mix well and refrigerate for at least 1 hour before serving, then sprinkle with chopped parsley and serve immediately.

Serves 4

Insalata di Pomodori e Basilico

Tomato and Basil Salad

Fresh basil and ripe tomatoes make one of the most appealing food combinations in Italian cooking. Grow your own, or buy the best possible from your favorite Italian grocery.

Ingredients	Regular	Metric
Olive oil	4 oz.	125 ml
Red wine vinegar	2 oz.	50 ml
Garlic cloves, minced	2	2
Basil leaves, chopped	3	3
Salt	1/2 tsp.	2 ml
Pepper	Pinch	Pinch
Tomatoes	6	6
Green pepper, sliced thinly	1	1
Green onions, sliced	2	2

1. Whisk the oil, vinegar, garlic, basil, salt and pepper together.
2. Slice the tomatoes, or cut in wedges if you prefer. Put them in a salad bowl with the green pepper and green onions.
3. Add the dressing and toss well, then put in the refrigerator for at least 1 hour before serving.

Serves 4

Basil/Basilico

Basil gets its name from the Greek word for king. The Greeks thought so much of this herb that they called it royal, and only kings were allowed to harvest it.

Today, anyone with a small plot of land, or even a patio container, can grow a summer crop of sweet-smelling basil with a minimum of effort and a maximum amount of enjoyment.

Although basil goes well with seafood, fowl, pork, lamb, veal, egg dishes, carrots, squash and green beans, its almost miraculous affinity for tomatoes, and its use in the famous Genoese pesto sauce make it one of the most prized of Italian herbs.

Buy it or grow it, and then preserve for later use by using the following methods:

1). Wash and dry fresh leaves, then put in a food processor or blender with just enough olive oil to make a smooth paste. Freeze in separate plastic containers. This can later be used for pesto or for any recipe which calls for fresh basil.

2). Wash and dry fresh leaves and put in a jar covered with olive oil. Cap tightly and refrigerate. The leaves will last up to six months this way, and the oil will be good too.

Insalata di Spinacie Canadese

Spinach Salad Canadian Style

Spinach is always cooked in Italy, which is a shame as raw spinach makes a delicious salad. Here is the recipe for this crisp, nutritious salad as it is served in North America.

Ingredients	Regular	Metric
Fresh spinach leaves	1 lb.	500 g
Bacon or pancetta slices, chopped	4	4
Mushrooms, sliced	1 cup	250 ml
Olive oil	4 oz.	125 ml
Lemon juice	2 oz.	50 ml
Wine vinegar	2 oz.	50 ml
Salt	1/2 tsp.	2 ml
Pepper	Pinch	Pinch
Egg, beaten	1	1
Hard-cooked egg, chopped	1	1

1. Wash the spinach leaves thoroughly and break off the hard stems. Drain and break into bite-size pieces, then place in a large bowl.
2. Cook the bacon in a frying pan for 3-5 minutes until crisp, then remove and drain.
3. Add bacon to the spinach along with the sliced mushrooms.
4. In other bowl, combine the oil, lemon juice, vinegar, salt and pepper, and whisk in the beaten egg until the mixture is thick and smooth.
4. Pour the dressing over the salad, toss well, and decorate with chopped egg before serving.

Serves 4-6

➤ *Make garlic oil by placing two peeled cloves of garlic in a jar with one cup of good quality olive oil. Cover and let stand for a day or two, then remove cloves. This oil can be made in quantity, and used for cooking and salad dressings.*

Insalata di Pasta

Macaroni Salad

In this salad, you can use any of the short-cut macaroni such as ziti, pennine, magliette or bocconcini.

Ingredients	Regular	Metric
Macaroni pasta	8 oz.	250 ml
Juice of 1 lemon		
Sweet red pepper, chopped	1	1
Celery stalk, diced	1	1
Mustard	1 tsp.	5 ml
Mayonnaise	2 tbsp.	30 ml
Olive oil	2 tbsp.	30 ml
Vinegar	2 tbsp.	30 ml
Salt	1/2 tsp.	2 ml
Pepper	Pinch	Pinch
Boiled eggs, sliced	2	2
Tomatoes, cut in wedges	2	2

1. Cook and drain the pasta, then chill.
2. Mix the next 9 ingredients together in a bowl, add cooled pasta and toss well.
3. Arrange on a serving platter and garnish with egg slices and tomato wedges.

Serves 4

▶ *Always keep mayonnaise, and foods containing mayonnaise, completely refrigerated until ready to eat, or else very sore stomachs or even illness could result. This is especially important to remember if you're going on a picnic on a nice sunny day.*

▶ *Hard-boiled eggs are easy to peel if they are still warm. Plunge the cooked eggs into cold water and shake back and forth for a moment, then crack the shells and remove them gently. Place the peeled eggs back in a bowl of cold water, and leave unrefrigerated until ready to use. They will keep for up to twenty-four hours, but don't chill them or they will become tough.*

DESSERTS
Dolci

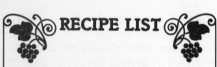
We Italians love to end our meals simply, with fine cheeses, fruit — either fresh or cooked in wine — and sweet nuts, especially almonds. Of course, we love a cup of strong, dark coffee too. Richer desserts are usually served at the end of a special dinner, but whatever the occasion, our desserts are very easy to make, including Zabaglione — the custard made with Marsala which is probably the most famous of all Italian desserts.

Crespelle

Italian Pancakes

There is a popular and truthful saying in cooking—"The first pancake nevers turns out." Just throw it away and keep on going, as the results with all the others will be well worth the effort.

Ingredients	Regular	Metric
Eggs	2	2
Flour	4 oz.	125 ml
Oil or melted butter	2 tbsp.	30 ml
Milk	6 oz.	200 ml

1. Beat the eggs in a bowl while you slowly add first the flour, then the oil or butter. Continue to beat until mixture thickens.
2. Stir in the milk until the batter has the consistency of heavy cream.
3. Grease a small frying pan and place it over medium heat.
4. When pan is hot, pour in 1 large spoonful of batter, and turn the pan until the bottom is evenly coated.
6. Cook until the edges of the pancake begin to curl, then shake the pan to loosen and turn the pancake over. Cook until lightly browned, then remove and start on the next one. Continue until all the batter is used up.
7. Serve immediately, or refrigerate until ready to use.

Makes 10-14

Crespelle con Ciliegie

Pancakes in Cherry Sauce

Crepes Suzette was the inspiration for this delicious cherry dessert. Try it with a scoop of vanilla ice cream for a different taste experience.

Ingredients	Regular	Metric
Sugar	4 tbsp.	60 ml
Pitted cherries, with juice	1 cup	250 ml
Sweet butter	3 tbsp.	45 ml
Cooked crespelles	8	8
Cherry brandy	2 oz.	50 ml
Brandy	3 oz.	75 ml

1. Melt sugar in a frying pan until golden.
2. Mash cherries in their juice, and add to the pan along with the butter.
3. Cook the mixture until it has the consistency of honey.
4. Fold crespelles in half twice, forming triangles. Put them into the sauce and pour in the liqueur and brandy. Flame, and spoon sauce over crespelles until they are saturated. Serve at once.

Serves 4-6

Crespelle

These thin, light pancakes are just one of the Italian culinary creations adopted by the French, and now known more commonly as *crepes.*

They are very versatile, and can be used for desserts, or filled with various savory stuffings and served as a main course. If they are going to be used as a sweet, you can add 2 tablespoons of powdered sugar to the batter before cooking.

➤ *When making crespelles, cover the batter and let stand for a couple of hours before using. The flour will be able to absorb some of the liquid and expand, making a lighter pancake.*

Espresso

Caffé Espresso is an Italian coffee which is enjoyed daily in most European countries, and is rapidly gaining popularity in North America. It differs from other coffees, because it must be made in a specific machine which works on the "steam pressure" principle. These espresso machines, which range from simple stove-top devices to the more elaborate and expensive ones, can be bought in specialty shops and most major department stores, and usually come with full instructions and recipes.

When buying your coffee, choose dark-roasted espresso beans, and either have them ground in the shop very finely, or grind them at home yourself as you go along. Don't let the grind become too powdery, though, or sticky sediment will seep into the cups. For convenience, you can buy ready-ground coffee, but make sure it has espresso written on the package.

Because the steam going through the grounds is so much hotter than boiling water, good espresso should have the consistency of table cream, and although it is wonderful on its own, it is often served with a liqueur added. Try adding a dash of Sambuca, Strega, or brandy, and serve after dinner, or anytime you wish.

► *Espresso coffee can be made from any dark-roasted beans, including the French variety, but the taste won't be the same as the Italian.*

Della Dominica

Sweet Pizza

Pizza doesn't always have to have tomatoes and cheese on top— sometimes it can be made with sweet ingredients for a delicious and different dessert.

Ingredients	Regular	Metric
Pizza dough	1 lb.	500 g
Lemon rind, grated	1 tbsp.	15 ml
Sugar	3 tbsp.	45 ml
Olive oil	2 tbsp.	30 ml
Egg yolk	1	1
Sweet white wine	6 oz.	200 ml
Milk	2 tbsp.	30 ml
Butter	1 tbsp.	15 ml
Breadcrumbs	1 cup	250 ml
Egg, beaten	1	1
Icing sugar	2 tbsp.	30 ml

1. Let pizza dough rise for 1 hour, then punch down and knead.
2. Gradually knead in the lemon rind, sugar, oil, egg yolk, wine and, if necessary, a little milk. The dough should be perfectly smooth, but not stiff. Work it until it is light and springy and comes away from the pastry board in one piece.
3. Butter a deep, wide cake pan and sprinkle with breadcrumbs. Add dough and press to fill the pan. Cover with a cloth and let rise again for 1 hour.
4. Brush top with beaten egg, then put in a preheated 375°F./190°C oven and bake for 50 minutes.
5. Remove and sprinkle with icing sugar before serving.

Serves 4-6

► *Freeze extra egg whites in ice cube trays, one white to a cube, then remove them to a plastic bag and store in the freezer until ready to use.*

Zabaglione

Hot Italian Custard

This is the most famous of all Italian desserts—a simple custard made glorious with the addition of Marsala wine.

Ingredients	Regular	Metric
Egg yolks	4	4
Sugar	4 tbsp.	60 ml
Marsala	3 oz.	75 ml
Lemon juice	2 tbsp.	30 ml

1. Whisk egg yolks in the top of a double boiler until creamy yellow.
2. Place over hot but not boiling water, and gradually whisk in other ingredients.
3. Continue to whisk vigorously until custard begins to thicken, then serve immediately—by itself or with fruit.

Serves 4

Granita di Limone

Lemon Ice

Italian lemon ice is sweet yet tart, and very refreshing. A food processor grinds the ice crystals very fine, and makes preparation much easier.

Ingredients	Regular	Metric
Water	4 cups	1 L
Sugar	1 1/2 cups	375 ml
Lemon rind, finely grated	2 tbsp.	30 ml
Lemon juice	1 cup	250 ml

1. Put water and sugar in a pan and bring to a boil. Lower the heat, stir in the lemon rind, and cook for 5 minutes.
2. Strain the liquid into a bowl and let cool at room temperature. Discard the lemon rind.
3. Stir in the lemon juice and place in ice trays in the freezer.
4. When mixture is frozen, remove from the freezer. If it is very hard, let soften slightly, then grind in a food processor using the blades.
5. When mixture is a smooth puree, put in serving bowls and serve immediately.

Serves 4-6

Granita di Fragole

Strawberry Ice

Make this cool and elegant ice as instructed in this recipe, or look at the recipe for Lemon Ice for the method of using a food processor to create a different consistency.

Ingredients	Regular	Metric
Water	2 cups	500 ml
Sugar	1 1/4 cups	325 ml
Strawberries	2 cups	500 ml

1. Put water and sugar in a pot and boil moderately for 15 minutes.
2. Mash hulled strawberries and strain through a colander.
3. Add syrup to berries and force mixture through a fine sieve.
4. This mixture may then be frozen in a hand-turned or electric freezer, or in a deep tray in the refrigerator freezer. In the last case, it will be necessary to beat the ice several times as it is freezing, using a hand or electric beater.

Serves 4

Liqueurs/Liquore

Italian liqueurs include some of the world's finest. They are delicious as a substitute for dessert if you have eaten too much, or served after dinner with a cup of fine Italian coffee.

Amaretto. A very popular liqueur with the flavor of almonds. It is sweet, amber-colored, and is usually served straight.

Grappa. This is a type of brandy, but it is not as smooth as some of the better Italian brandies. The fact that it is traditionally made from the pressed grape skins accounts for its more earthy quality.

Marsala. A fortified wine, amber in color. Its sweet flavor, reminiscent of almonds or cherries, makes it a great favorite for cooking as well as drinking.

Sambuca. This is a clear liqueur which tastes like liquorice, and is often served flamed with a whole coffee bean in the bottom of the glass.

Strega. This word means *witch* but I'm not sure how it applies to the drink. It is a yellow, sweet liqueur with a citrus flavor, and is very popular.

Ricotta

Ricotta is a curdy cheese very similar to cottage cheese, except that ricotta is made from goat or sheep milk, and is a bit creamier. It can be used in a variety of dishes, as well as being sprinkled with sugar and eaten for dessert.

► *For maximum volume in beaten egg whites, always have them at room temperature, and then add a pinch of salt just at the end of whipping.*

Cannoli di Ricotta

Ricotta Cream Rolls

Cannoli is a very popular dessert in Italy which you can buy at any good Italian bakery. To make them at home, you'll need several metal tubes about ½"/1 cm in diameter, and about 6"/15 cm long, so the pastry will hold its shape while deep-frying.

Ingredients	Regular	Metric
Flour	3 cups	750 ml
Sugar	4 tbsp.	60 ml
Cinnamon	1 tsp.	5 ml
Shortening	4 tbsp.	60 ml
Eggs, beaten	2	2
Water	1 oz.	50 ml
Ricotta cheese	1 lb.	500 g
Sugar	1 cup	250 ml
Vanilla	1 tsp.	5 ml
Peel of 1 lemon, grated		
Oil for deep-frying		

1. Mix the flour, sugar and cinnamon together in a bowl, and cut in the shortening until the mixture is fine.
2. Add beaten eggs, reserving 2 tablespoons, and blend into flour and shortening, then add just enough water to make a smooth ball of dough.
3. Knead for 1 minute, then chill until ready to use.
4. Roll dough into a fairly thin sheet, and cut into 3" × 5" squares.
5. Roll the squares around the metal tubes and seal the edges with beaten egg.

6. Heat the oil to 375°F./190°C and cook rolls until golden brown all over. Drain on paper towels and cool, then remove the metal tubes.
7. Combine cheese, sugar, vanilla and lemon rind together, and fill rolls with this mixture. Place on a platter, sprinkle with a little icing sugar and serve.

Makes about 16 rolls

Tortiere del Pastore

Ricotta Cheese Pie

This is an Italian version of cheesecake. If you always use fresh ricotta, the pie will always have a heavenly light and creamy texture.

Ingredients	Regular	Metric
Ricotta cheese	2 lbs.	1 kg
Grated peel for 1 orange		
Grated peel from 1 lemon		
Flour	6 tbsp.	90 ml
Vanilla	1 tsp.	5 ml
Eggs	4	4
Sugar	1 1/2 cups	375 ml
Powdered sugar	1 tbsp.	15 ml
Pre-made 9"/22 cm pie shell	1	1

1. In one bowl, combine the cheese with the orange and lemon peels, and stir in the flour and vanilla.
2. In another bowl, beat the eggs and slowly add the sugar. Continue beating until the mixture is foamy.
3. Stir into the cheese mixture, then pour this into the pie shell.
4. Bake pie in a preheated 350°F./180°C oven for 1 hour, or until the filling is firm. Sprinkle with powdered sugar, cut into wedges, and serve.

Serves 4-6

Ricotta al Caffè

This is a beautiful dessert which can be made very easily, and serves about four people.
    2 cups ricotta cheese
    6 tablespoons castor sugar
    2 tablespoons finely ground coffee
    4 tablespoons rum
Stir until smooth, refrigerate, and serve with cream and wafers.

Capuccino

Capuccino is a combination of espresso coffee and hot milk. Ideally, the milk should not only be hot but steamed, and good espresso machines have metal arms which are inserted into the milk to steam it until it froths. Then an equal amount of espresso is added, and the drink is served with cinnamon or nutmeg on top, or for something special, a sprinkling of shaved chocolate.

Pere Cotte al Vino

Poached Pears in Red Wine

Italians love fresh fruit cooked in wine. When fresh pears aren't available, canned halves are very good prepared this way as long as the cooking time is cut in half.

Ingredients	Regular	Metric
Pears	4	4
Juice of 1 lemon		
Juice of 1 orange		
Red wine	2 cups	500 ml
Sugar	4 oz.	125 ml
Cinnamon stick	1	1

1. Preheat oven to 375°F./180°C.
2. Peel pears, cut in half and remove the cores.
3. Combine other ingredients in a baking dish and mix well. Place pear halves in a single layer in the dish and cook in the oven for 45-60 minutes, turning and basting often.
4. When pears are tender, remove the cinnamon stick, and refrigerate pears in syrup until ready to serve.

Serves 4-6

Pane di Pasqua

Italian Easter Bread

Sweet egg breads are traditionally baked for Easter celebrations, but this is such a delicious recipe that you'll want to prepare it all year long.

Ingredients	Regular	Metric
Active dry yeast	3 packets	3
Milk, lukewarm	4 oz.	125 ml
Flour, all-purpose	9 cups	2.25 L
Salt	1/4 tsp.	1 ml
Eggs, beaten	6	6
Sugar	1 cup	250 ml

Butter, melted and cooled	1 cup	250 ml
Raisins	4 oz.	125 ml
Orange peel, grated	4 tbsp.	60 ml
Egg, beaten for glaze	1	1

1. Dissolve the yeast in a little milk.
2. Sift 2 cups of flour into a large bowl, then add salt and yeast and enough milk to make a smooth dough. Cover and let rise for 1 hour.
3. Punch dough down and work in half the eggs, half the sugar, 2½ cups of the flour, and half the melted butter. Knead vigorously until the dough is smooth and no longer sticky, then place back in the bowl, cover, and let rise for 2 hours.
4. Punch down the dough and work in the remaining flour, eggs, sugar and butter. Then add raisins and orange peel and knead until smooth. Put back in bowl, cover, and let rise for 5 hours.
5. Punch dough down, knead lightly, and shape into 2 loaves. Place on buttered baking sheet, brush with beaten egg, and leave to rise for the last time.
6. Preheat oven to 400°.F/200°C and bake bread for 30-40 minutes, or until loaves are well-risen and golden brown.

Makes 2 loaves

Easter/Pasqua

Easter is a very important religious and social festival in Italy in which food plays a big part. Not only is it the end of forty days of Lenten fasting, but a time when the whole family and all the relatives come together to eat and have a good time. Much of the food is symbolic, with origins going back to the pagan days of Europe when spring was celebrated as a new beginning, but the traditional new young lamb is always served as a remembrance of the Lamb of God.

Egg bread is usually eaten in the morning. The eggs not only signify the Resurrection, but also symbolize fertility and rebirth, and the bread gives the promise of a bountiful summer.

Apricot/Albicocche

If you can find fresh apricots, choose ones with a smooth skin, golden-yellow with a pinkish tinge, and use as soon as they are ripe. For most North Americans outside of California, fresh apricots are hard to get except in early summer, but many people believe that this fruit tastes better canned or dried. This way, it's available all year long.

Dried apricots can be eaten just the way they are, and are prized as an excellent source of fiber and Vitamin A. For cooking, however, you should soak them in cold water for several hours until they soften up, then use in a recipe, or simmer in water and sugar. Apricots make a wonderful jam — try brushing it on tarts and pies before baking for a tasty and shiny glaze — a lovely butter, and a delicious brandy.

Gelato Fritto con Salsa d'Apricotte

Fried Ice Cream with Apricot Sauce

Don't be afraid that the ice cream will melt—the batter and the cake will protect it, but don't take too long! Serve this dish pronto!

Ingredients	Regular	Metric
Eggs	2	2
Flour	2 tbsp.	30 ml
Sugar	6 tbsp.	90 ml
Oil	1 tbsp.	15 ml
Water	4 oz.	125 ml
Baking powder	1 tsp.	5 ml
Milk	2 oz.	50 ml
Sweet butter	4 tbsp.	60 ml
Juice of 2 oranges		
Juice of 2 lemons		
Apricots, chopped	1 cup	250 ml
Brandy	2 oz	50 ml
Sponge cake loaf	1	1
Vanilla ice cream	1 cup	250 ml
Oil for frying		

1. To make batter, mix the eggs, flour, 2 tablespoons of sugar, oil, water, baking powder and milk, very thoroughly in a bowl, then let sit for 10 minutes or until ready to use.
2. Heat the rest of the sugar in a frying pan. When it turns golden, add the butter, orange and lemon juices, apricots and brandy. Cook for several minutes, then set aside.
3. Cut sponge cake into 4 horizontal pieces so that each slice is 10"/25 cm by 2"/5 cm. Put equal amount of ice cream on each slice, roll the cake around the ice cream, and put in the freezer to harden.
4. Heat oil to 375°F./190°C. Dip the rolls in batter until well-coated, and deep-fry until golden brown, then remove and drain.
5. Heat apricot sauce, pour over rolls, and serve immediately.

Serves 4

Zuppa Inglese

Italian Rum Cake

A beautiful dessert with layers of pound cake, fruit, rum and creamy custard, covered with whipped cream and almonds. A wonderful party dish.

Ingredients	Regular	Metric
Mixed fruits, chopped	4 cups	1 L
Sugar	4 oz.	125 ml
Rum	6 oz.	200 ml
Egg yolks	6	6
Pound cake	12 oz.	375 g
Strawberry jam	4 oz.	125 ml
Heavy cream	6 oz.	200 ml
Candied fruit, chopped	4 oz.	125 ml
Slivered almonds	4 oz.	125 ml

1. Prepare mixed fruits by cutting up favorite fruit in season, and mixing with 2 tablespoons of sugar and 2 tablespoons of rum. Chill until ready to use.
2. Place egg yolks in the top of a double boiler or a large bowl, and set over hot but not boiling water. Add remaining sugar and whisk vigorously until egg yolks are pale and thick.
3. Continue whisking and gradually add 2 oz./50 ml of rum, then cook and whisk until custard has doubled in volume and is soft and fluffy. Put bowl over ice-water and stir until mixture has cooled.
4. Cut the cake into medium-thin slices and arrange a layer in the bottom of a large glass bowl. Sprinkle with rum, then cover lightly with jam. Put some of the fruit on top, and then a generous amount of custard. Continue layers until bowl is almost full, ending with cake. Chill until ready to use.
5. Whip cream and spread on top, then sprinkle with candied fruit and almonds and serve.

Serves 8-10

Zuppa Inglese

This dish is not a soup at all, but a very popular Italian dessert. *Zuppa* may come from the word "sop", meaning bread or cake soaked in liquid.

It is called *inglese* because it is based on the English dessert called trifle or tipsy pudding, and because of the rum sprinkled on top of the cake. In Italy, many recipes which contain rum are dubbed *inglese*, as British sailors were famous for their fondness for it.

Struffoli

Neopolitan Honey Balls

These delicacies can be shaped into a pyramid and kept for up to a week. They are wonderful for Christmas or any special occasion.

Ingredients	Regular	Metric
Flour	3 cups	750 ml
Salt	1/2 tsp.	2 ml
Cinnamon	1/4 tsp.	1 ml
Eggs	4	4
Oil for frying		
Honey	12 oz.	375 ml
Sugar	4 oz.	125 ml

1. Sift flour, salt and cinnamon into large bowl. Make a well in the center and add the eggs, then mix with your fingers, adding another egg if necessary, until you have a smooth dough. Knead well and place under an inverted bowl.
2. Heat 2"/5 cm of oil in a large frying pan.
3. Break off some of the dough and roll it until it is $^1/_2$"/1 cm thick. Cut into $^1/_4$"/$^1/_2$ cm pieces.
4. When oil is hot, add the pieces and cook until golden. Remove and drain on paper towels, and continue until all the dough is used.
5. Heat the honey in a saucepan until it becomes thin, then put struffoli in a bowl and drizzle honey over the top. Sprinkle sugar over all, and toss until honey and sugar are distributed evenly.
6. Wet your hands and shape struffoli into a pyramid.

Makes about 4 dozen

Pesche Ripiene

Stuffed Peaches

Cooked fruits are always popular at the end of an Italian meal, and this one is especially good. Juicy peaches are split in half, then filled with a delicious macaroon stuffing and baked in the oven. When fresh fruit isn't available, canned halves are fine, as long as you cut the cooking time in half.

Italian Cheeses/Formaggio

Italian cheeses are my favorites, naturally, and there are many, many different kinds. Especially popular are the grating cheeses such as parmesan, romano and provolone piccante, and those used often in cooking such as fontina, mozzarella, gorgonzola and ricotta.

For eating alone, or with fruit as the perfect end to a meal, try some of these types and you will be pleasantly surprised.

Asiago. This is a medium sharp cheese which is beautiful when eaten with fruit after dinner, or as a snack. It has a slightly smoky taste, and is made from partially skimmed cow's milk.

Auricchio is a very strong and sharp cheese similar to provolone piccante. It is excellent for eating, but it may be a bit too strong for cooking. It is easily recognizable as it comes in huge pear-shaped and waxed balls hanging on ropes.

Ingredients	Regular	Metric
Peaches	4	4
Butter	4 tbsp.	60 ml
Sugar	3 tbsp.	45 ml
Macaroons, crumbled	4 oz.	125 ml
Egg yolk, beaten	1	1
Amaretto liqueur	2 oz.	50 ml
Water or white wine	2 oz.	50 ml
Almonds, peeled	8	8

1. Blanch peaches in boiling water for 2 minutes. Plunge into cold water and remove skins, then cut in half and remove pits.
2. Carefully scoop out some of the peach pulp from each half, leaving a shell 1"/2 cm thick. Mash pulp and reserve.
3. Cream together 2 tablespoons of the butter and 2 tablespoons of sugar.
4. Add macaroon crumbs, peach pulp, egg yolk and liqueur, and mix well.
5. Fill peach halves with this mixture, then place them in a buttered baking dish with the water or wine in the bottom.
6. Dot each peach half with the remaining butter and place an almond on top. Sprinkle remaining sugar on the almond only, and bake in a preheated 350°F./180°C oven for 30 minutes (15 minutes for canned peach halves) until tender but still firm. Serve hot or cold.

Serves 4

Bel Paese. Most of Italy's cheeses have been around for some time, for up to a thousand years in many cases, but bel paese is a relative newcomer. It was developed in the early 1900's, and has since become much sought after for its soft texture and mild, delicate flavor. A lovely dessert cheese.

Crotonese. This is a beautiful drawn-curd cheese made of sheep and goat's milk in Crotone in Calabria. Its slightly peppery taste makes it a nice cheese to eat at the end of a meal with fruit.

Caciocavallo is a cheese made in several regions in Italy. It has been made since the 4th century, and got its name from the way it is aged. After the cheese is churned from whole or partially skimmed cow's milk, it is hung in pairs on poles to dry. Thus its name – "cheese on horseback". It is good to eat with red wine, and very fine in baked dishes like lasagne.

> *"One of the most important things in cooking and eating is variety. To be bored by food is to be bored by life."*

Macedonia di Frutta Fresca

Fresh Fruit Cocktail

This is a good dessert to use for company or at a party. The recipe calls for grapes, pears, peaches, bananas and cantaloupe, but any kind of fruit may be used.

Ingredients	Regular	Metric
Sugar	2 oz.	50 ml
Butter, unsalted	2 tbsp.	30 ml
Sherry or Marsala	2 oz.	50 ml
Brandy	2 tbsp.	30 ml
Juice of 2 oranges		
Juice of 2 lemons		
Seedless grapes	1 cup	250 g
Pears, cored and chopped	2	2
Bananas, peeled and sliced	2	2
Peaches, peeled, stoned and sliced	2	2
Cantaloupe, peeled, seeded and chopped	1	1

1. Melt sugar in a frying pan and when it turns gold, add the butter.
2. When butter has melted, add sherry, brandy and juices. Simmer for 2 minutes until liquid has reduced a little.

3. Combine fruit in a large bowl and pour in the sauce, then toss to mix well.
4. Serve in fruit dishes, with ice cream or whipped cream.

Serves 6-8

Mele Dolce

Apple Fritters

Fruit cooked in sweet batter is popular in many countries. This version is from Northern Italy.

Ingredients	Regular	Metric
Apples	4	4
Sugar	1 cup	250 ml
Rum or other liquor	5 tbsp.	75 ml
Eggs, separated	2	2
Milk	6 oz.	200 ml
Flour	6 tbsp.	90 ml
Salt	Pinch	Pinch
Oil for frying		

1. Core and peel apples, then slice into donut-shaped rounds. Put into a large bowl with 3/4 cup of sugar, and rum or other liquor. Cover and let apples marinate for 2-3 hours, stirring occasionally.
2. Whisk egg yolks and add milk, then gradually sift in flour, mixing constantly.
3. In another bowl, beat egg whites and salt until stiff, then fold into the batter.
4. Pour oil 2"/5 cm deep into large saucepan or deep fryer, and heat to 375°F./190°C.
5. Dip apple rounds into the batter and lower them one at a time into the oil. Turn over, and when golden on both sides, remove with a slotted spoon and drain on paper towels.
6. Arrange fritters on a platter, sprinkle with remaining sugar and serve.

Serves 4-6

▶ *When combining a heavy mixture with beaten egg whites, always fold the mixture into the whites — heavy to light. Less air will be forced out of the whites this way.*

Cassata Gelata

Cassata Ice Cream

For nice individual servings, use a muffin pan to freeze the ice cream.

Ingredients	Regular	Metric
Egg yolks beaten	4	4
Sugar	4 oz.	125 ml
Lemon rind	2 tbsp.	30 ml
Vanilla extract	1/2 tsp.	2 ml
Milk	1 1/2 cups	375 ml
Heavy cream	1 cup	250 ml
Candied fruit	2 oz.	50 ml
Almonds	4 oz.	125 ml

➤ *If cream is well-chilled, you can count on it doubling in volume when whipped.*

1. Beat the egg yolks with the sugar, lemon rind and vanilla until smooth and thickened, then stir in the milk.
2. Cook over low heat, or in a double boiler, stirring constantly until the mixture thickens into a smooth custard.
3. Transfer to a cool bowl and place in the freezer. While the mixture is freezing, stir several times to break up the ice crystals.
4. Chill a dessert mold or metal bowl with a rounded bottom. Sprinkle the bottom with half the almonds, then line the inside with the frozen custard, leaving a large cavity in the center. Return to the freezer.
5. Whip the cream into soft peaks, then stir in the candied fruit and the remaining almonds. Fill the cavity with this mixture to the top of the bowl. Cover with plasic wrap and return to the freezer to harden.
6. When ready to serve, lower the bowl into hot water for several seconds, then turn upside down on serving plate, lift off bowl and slice the ice.

Serves 4-6

Budino di Riso al Canadese

Rice Pudding Canadian Style

The maple syrup adds a Canadian touch to this popular Italian dessert. I hope you enjoy it.

Ingredients	Regular	Metric
Milk	3 cups	750 ml
Rice	1 cup	250 ml
Sugar	4 tbsp.	60 ml
Cinnamon	1 tsp.	5 ml
Nutmeg	Pinch	Pinch
Whipping cream	1 cup	250 ml
Maple syrup	1 cup	250 ml

1. Heat milk in a medium pot, and when it starts to boil, add rice and cover. Lower the heat and cook for 30 minutes without stirring.
2. When the rice is tender, add sugar, cinnamon and nutmeg, then let cool.
3. Whip cream into soft peaks and fold into the mixture gently. Pour into individual dishes.
4. Put maple syrup into a pan and heat until thin, then pour on top of pudding and serve.

Serves 4-6

Almond/Mandorla

The almond is a delicious nut and a close relative of the peach. It comes in two varieties, sweet and bitter — the sweet is the one we use for eating and cooking. If almonds are going to be used in a recipe, it is best to buy them unroasted and still in the shell for absolute freshness.

They are wonderful with fish and vegetables . . . slivered and cooked with butter. Roasted or fresh, they are a popular snack with drinks, a custom which may date back 2000 years to the Romans, who believed that if they ate almonds while drinking alcohol, they wouldn't get tipsy. They might have been slightly mixed-up if they had been imbibing Amaretto, a popular almond liqueur. It's not to be confused with *amaretti* or macaroons. These delicious little cakes were invented in Italy, and brought to France in the 16th century, where they became very popular.

Today, Italian macaroons are made in many sizes including one the very size of an almond, a specialty of Salsamaggiore in Parma.

Amaretti Dolci

Sweet Almond Macaroons

Amaretti are cookies traditionally made with bitter almonds, but here is a sweet version which is very easy to make.

Ingredients	Regular	Metric
Almonds, peeled	1 1/2 cups	375 ml
Egg whites	2	2
Salt	1/4 tsp.	1 ml
Sugar	1 1/2 cup	375 ml
Vanilla extract	1/4 tsp.	1 ml
Almond extract	1/4 tsp.	1 ml

1. Put almonds into a blender and grind into a powder.
2. Beat egg whites with the salt until fluffy, then beat in sugar, one spoonful at a time, until stiff peaks are formed.
3. Fold in ground almonds, vanilla and almond extract. Drop from a teaspoon onto a well-greased cookie sheet, about 1"/2 cm apart.
4. Bake in a preheated 350°F./180°C oven for 10-15 minutes, or until very lightly browned.

Makes 3 dozen

Index